AMERICAN VOICES FROM

The Wild West

AMERICAN VOICES FROM

The Wild West

Rebecca Stefoff

Marshall Cavendish
Benchmark

New York

Marshall Cavendish Benchmark
99 White Plains Road
Tarrytown, New York 10591-9001
www.marshallcavendish.us

Library of Congress Cataloging-in-Publication Data
Stefoff, Rebecca, 1951–
The Wild West / by Rebecca Stefoff.
p. cm. — (American voices from—)
Summary: "Presents the history of the Wild West through a variety of primary source images and documents, such as diary entries, newspaper accounts, public speeches, popular literature, and personal letters"—Provided by publisher.
Includes bibliographical references and index.
ISBN-13: 978-0-7614-2170-2
ISBN-10: 0-7614-2170-X
1. West (U.S.)—History—19th century—Juvenile literature. 2. West (U.S.)—History—19th century—Sources—Juvenile literature. I. Title. II. Series.
F591.S8228 2007   978'.02—dc22   2005028192

Printed in Malaysia
1 3 5 6 4 2

Editor: Joyce Stanton
Editorial Director: Michelle Bisson
Art Director: Anahid Hamparian
Series design and composition: Anne Scatto / PIXEL PRESS
Photo Research by Linda Sykes Picture Research, Inc., Hilton Head, S.C.

ON THE COVER: *The Deputy Sheriff*, by Frank Tenney Johnson, 1929

ON THE TITLE PAGE: *The Coming and Going of the Pony Express*, by Frederic Remington, 1900. As a weary rider prepares to unsaddle his exhausted horse, a fresh horse and rider spring forward, carrying mail for the Pony Express, which became a symbol of western adventure.

Acknowledgments

The author is grateful to the reference staff of the Art, Literature, and History Departments of the Multnomah County Library, Portland, Oregon, for their invaluable help in locating materials and checking sources, and to the library staff of the Oregon Historical Society, also in Portland, Oregon.

Contents

The Spanish-American or Mexican vaquero was the original cowboy. Although vaqueros did not often wear clothes as showy as those in this nineteenth-century painting, their hats, boots, saddles, and other gear were copied across the American West.

About Primary Sources

What Is a Primary Source?

In the pages that follow, you will be hearing many different "voices" from a special time in America's past. Some of the selections are long and others are short. You'll find many easy to understand at first reading, while others may require several readings. All the selections have one thing in common, however. They are primary sources. That is the name historians give to the bits and pieces of information that make up the record of human existence. Primary sources are important to us because they are the core material of all historical investigation. You might call them "history" itself.

Primary sources are evidence; they give historians the all-important clues they need to understand the past. Perhaps you have read a detective story in which a sleuth must solve a mystery by piecing together bits of evidence he or she uncovers. The detective makes deductions, or educated guesses based on the evidence, and solves the mystery once all the deductions point in a certain direction. Historians work in much the same way. Like detectives, historians analyze data through careful reading and rereading.

Amos Bad Heart Bull (1869–1913) of the Oglala Sioux filled a discarded army ledger with 415 paintings that documented his people's daily life and history. This image of the Battle of the Little Bighorn in 1876 includes a portrait of the artist's cousin, Crazy Horse.

After much analysis, historians draw conclusions about an event, a person, or an entire era. Individual historians may analyze the same evidence and come to different conclusions. That is why there is often sharp disagreement about an event.

Primary sources are also called *documents*. This rather dry word can be used to describe many different things: an official speech by a government leader, an old map, an act of Congress, a letter worn out from much handling, an entry hastily scrawled in a diary, a detailed newspaper account of an event, a funny or sad song, a colorful poster, a cartoon, an old painting, a faded photograph, or someone's remembrances captured on tape or film.

By examining the following documents, you, the reader, will be taking on the role of historian. Here is your chance to immerse yourself in a time and place that has become part of American history and legend—the Wild West. You'll meet people who lived and worked in the American West during the second half of the nineteenth century. They struggled with a challenging landscape, with an evolving social order, and with each other, and their conflicts defined the era that came to be called the Wild West. You'll also learn how the image of the Wild West was shaped and marketed by westerners themselves and by outsiders. Finally, you'll explore the influence of Wild West history and mythology on our shared culture.

Our language has changed since the nineteenth and early twentieth centuries. Some words and expressions will be unfamiliar to a

Photographers chronicled some of the events and characters of the West, such as this family of settlers—possibly Mormons—taking a rest during their trek to the frontier. By capturing a real moment in time, photos create primary sources in visual form.

person living in the early twenty-first century. Even familiar words may have been spelled differently when these materials were written. In addition, some of the primary sources in this book were written by people with limited education. Don't let the unfamiliar language discourage you! Trying to figure out language is exactly the kind of work a historian does. Like a historian, you will end with a deeper, more meaningful understanding of the past.

How to Read a Primary Source

Each document in this book deals with some aspect of the history and legends of the Wild West. Some of the documents are part of public or official history. These might include a newspaper article, a political speech, or a scene from a novel or play. Other documents, such as letters or journal entries, are drawn from the lives of ordinary people. All of these sources help us understand something about the Wild West—such as what it was like to live and work in that time and place, or what role the image of the Wild West has played in people's imaginations.

As you read each document, ask yourself some basic questions. Who is writing or speaking? Who is that person's audience? What is the writer's point of view? What is he or she trying to tell the audience? Is the message clearly expressed, or is it implied, that is, stated indirectly? What words does the writer use to convey his or her message? Are the words emotional or objective in tone? If you are looking at a newspaper cartoon, a photograph, or another work of art, examine it carefully, taking in all the details. What is happening in the foreground? In the background? What is its purpose? These are

New Englander Nathaniel Currier was one of the founders of Currier and Ives, a famous nineteenth-century publisher of illustrations. In 1849 Currier drew this mocking cartoon about the gold rush. It suggests that people were going to foolish lengths to get to California.

questions that can help you think critically about a primary source.

Some tools have been included with the documents to help you in your investigations. Unusual words have been defined near the selections. Thought-provoking questions follow the selections. They help focus your reading so you can get the most out of each document. As you read each selection, you'll probably come up with many questions of your own. That's great! The work of a historian always leads to many, many questions. Some can be answered, while others require more investigation. Perhaps when you finish this book, your questions will lead you to further explorations of the Wild West.

Painted for a post office in Helper, Utah, around 1939, this mural calls up images of western life that were already decades old.

Introduction

THE WILD WEST: HISTORY AND MYTHOLOGY

"I was raised in a little town of which most of you have never heard," Dwight D. Eisenhower, president of the United States, said in a speech in 1953. "But in the West it is a famous place. It is called Abilene, Kansas."

The president went on to tell his listeners a few things about Abilene. "We had as our marshal for a long time a man named Wild Bill Hickok," he said. "If you don't know anything about him, read your Westerns more. Now that town had a code, and I was raised as a boy to prize that code. It was: meet anyone face to face with whom you disagree. You could not sneak up on him from behind, or do any damage to him, without suffering the penalty of an enraged citizenry. If you met him face-to-face and took the same risks he did, you could get away with almost anything, as long as the bullet was in front."

Why did President Eisenhower mention Abilene and Wild Bill Hickok in that speech? At the time, he was furious about criticisms of his administration, attacks that he considered sly and underhanded. Eisenhower used his boyhood in Abilene and the town's connection with a famous Wild West marshal to illustrate the honorable way to fight, directly and openly. There were just two things wrong with Eisenhower's statement. First, James Butler Hickok, the gunslinger who became known as "Wild Bill," served as marshal of Abilene for less than a year, from April to December in 1871— "a single cattle season, during which he spent most of his time gambling," historian David Murdoch Hamilton points out in *The American West: The Invention of a Myth.* Marshal Hickok also drank alcohol every day and managed to shoot one of his own deputies by accident. Second, Hickok hadn't exactly lived by Eisenhower's straight-shooting, fair-playing "code of the West." In his first killing, ten years before he became marshal of Abilene, Hickok lay concealed in ambush to shoot an unarmed man.

Eisenhower was neither the first nor the last American president to make proud but somewhat mistaken references to the Wild West heritage. Ronald Reagan, president in the 1980s, frequently used images drawn from the nineteenth-century West to define America's greatness. Reagan, who had acted in such western films as *Santa Fe Trail* (1940) and *Cattle Queen of Montana* (1955), said in 1983, "Tales of Wild West men and women, from Kit Carson to Wild Bill Hickok, to Calamity Jane to Annie Oakley, are woven into the dreams of our youth and the standards we aim to live by as adults. Ideals of courageous and self-reliant heroes, both men and women, are the stuff of Western lore. . . ."

Statements such as Eisenhower's and Reagan's illustrate the values and virtues that many Americans associate with the Wild West, or the Old West. Yet the Wild West is as much legend, or "lore," as it is history. The history of the West has been glorified, sometimes almost beyond recognition, by passage of time, by the public's hunger for adventures and heroes, and by fiction, television, and movies. The four heroes Reagan mentioned are good examples. Hickok was occasionally a lawman and always an excellent marksman, but many episodes of his career were far from noble. And while the Old West had its share of genuinely heroic women, Martha Jane Canarry, nicknamed Calamity Jane, wasn't one of them. She created her own legend in a highly imaginative autobiography, in which she claimed to have worked as an official army scout for Lieutenant Colonel George Armstrong Custer. In reality, as Custer's orderly recorded, she was a pathetic vagrant who followed the troops, begging them for whiskey in exchange for doing their laundry; years later, she died of alcoholism. As for trick-shooter Annie Oakley, she really was a remarkably skilled markswoman, but she was not a western heroine: at the time she gained

As primary sources travel through time, they may be altered or doctored. This 1895 photograph, supposed to be of Calamity Jane, has been painted over with oil paint. For that reason it is not a completely reliable guide to how she looked.

fame as an entertainer, she had never been west of the Mississippi River. And although Christopher "Kit" Carson performed fearless deeds as an army scout and Indian fighter in the early days of the Wild West, his real-life exploits were sometimes overshadowed by the tall tales that journalists and others spun about him both before and after his death in 1868.

Behind legends lie historical truths, waiting to be uncovered. In recent years, historians have scraped away at the lore that encrusts the Wild West, revealing ever more of its true history. They are helping us to learn what the men and women who walked the dusty streets of towns such as Tombstone and Dodge City were really like. Sometimes, though, people value legends and myths for their own sake, as entertainment or as inspiration. This seems to be the case with tales and images of the Wild West. As entertainment, the Wild West offered a realm of adventure to which anyone could escape in imagination. As inspiration, it offered heroes whose behavior could be admired and imitated. Whatever their historical accuracy—or lack of it—the legends of the Wild West contain something that many Americans, from the late nineteenth century to the present day, have found fascinating or meaningful. They have became an American mythology.

What is the setting of that mythology? The phrase *Wild West* calls up images of cowboys and Indians, gold miners and gunfighters, campfires under the stars, and saloons with swinging doors through which, at any moment, a hard-eyed, dangerous stranger might walk—but what were the Wild West's outlines in space and time?

In geographic terms, the West was much more than the sagebrush and the red-rock mesas that have formed the background of

Actor William S. Hart (*center*, with pistols), star of many early western films, was one of the first to promote the connection between the Wild West and the movie business. Here he appears in a scene from *The Aryan* (1916), the story of an angry loner who is saved by a woman's love.

countless television shows and films. It included the Great Plains grasslands of Kansas and Nebraska as well as the deserts and mountains of the Far West. And beyond the familiar cattle roundups of Texas and the gunfights of Arizona were the mining camps of Montana and the Indian wars of Idaho.

The exploration of this vast region began long before the time of cowboys and gunfighters. Most people, though, think of the Old

An unknown nineteenth-century artist captured the isolation and wildness of Sutter's Mill, California, where the chance discovery of a few nuggets of precious metal set off the great gold rush of 1849—one of the events that marks the beginning of the Wild West era.

West or Wild West as falling within the second half of the nineteenth century. Two important events in 1848 set the stage for the era. The first of these events was the end of the Mexican War. Two years earlier, the United States had gone to war with its southern neighbor to win control of some of the former Spanish colonial territory that made up Mexico. (One of Mexico's northern provinces, Texas, had already broken away from the Mexican government; it became a U.S. state in 1845.) Under the Treaty of Guadalupe Hidalgo, which ended the war, Mexico gave to the United States an enormous tract of land that included California, Utah, Nevada, and parts of Arizona, New Mexico, Colorado, and Wyoming. Although the United States later added smaller acquisitions, the treaty essentially set the border of the American West and opened the region to U.S. settlement and development.

The second important event of 1848 was the discovery of gold at Sutter's Mill in California. That find kicked off the gold rush of 1849, the first of many gold and silver rushes that punctuated the history of the West with bursts of frenzied excitement and, occasionally, violence. The California gold rush brought thousands of people to the Far West. Few of them found fortunes in the goldfields, but many stayed to become part of the Western population. Another great gold rush, this one in 1899, can be seen as the end of the Wild West era. In the 1899 rush, hordes of hungry, hopeful prospectors struggled north to a new frontier: the Klondike region along Canada's Yukon River. By that time, the Wild West was well on its way to being settled and civilized. And the men and women who had left their mark on it were becoming larger-than-life literary characters and entertainers rather than flesh-and-blood people.

The historical forces that defined the Wild West created an environment of conflict and drama that is reflected in the Western mythology that developed over the years. The Mexican War lasted only two years, but it was the result of many years of tension in some parts of the West. A greater source of tension, and one that touched almost every part of the West, was the long history of strife between the Native American peoples and the settlers who slowly but relentlessly took over most of their land. That struggle reached its final stages in the Old West. There were other kinds of conflict as well. Before the Civil War, western territories on the verge of statehood saw bitter disputes between supporters and opponents of slavery. The Civil War itself spilled into the West. A few battles were fought on western territory, and after the war, former Confederate soldiers and freed blacks alike crossed the Mississippi, adding to the population of the frontier lands. As the settlement of the West proceeded, new conflicts appeared, such as the showdowns between outlaws and lawmen or the rivalry between small homesteaders and big-business cattle companies.

First a wilderness, then a frontier, the West eventually became part of civilized society, linked to the rest of the nation and to the world by telegraph wires and railroad tracks. The people of the Wild West had reshaped the land to suit new purposes, but in doing so, they brought about the end of the frontier. In the mythology of the Wild West, though, the frontier lives on.

At the heart of the myth is the rugged, noble hero—the "good guy" who fights to defend the weak and to protect the community. But because this hero is a loner, with a spirit that thrives in the

Ration Day at the Reservation, 1919, Joseph Henry Sharp. Born in Ohio and trained as an artist in Europe, Sharp (1859–1953) began traveling in Montana in the 1890s and later moved to New Mexico, where this somber scene was painted. Sharp's observations of Native American customs, clothing, and ceremonies were so detailed that historians and anthropologists now prize his paintings for their accurate portrayal of Indian cultures during the difficult transition into the modern world.

A brooding image of the solitary westerner from *The Virginian*, a best-selling novel that launched half a dozen movies and a television series. Together with *Shane*, it defined the Wild West hero: a rough but noble character who helps the weak and does the right thing even when others fail to understand or appreciate him.

wilderness, he cannot long live in settled, civilized surroundings. He must keep moving on, forever seeking a new frontier beyond the next horizon. In this way, the western myth celebrates both the epic survival qualities of strong individuals *and* the importance of building and preserving communities. Nowhere are these two themes more clearly shown than in one of the most popular western movies ever made, *Shane*. Released in 1953, *Shane* is the story of a wandering warrior, a gunfighter with a tortured past who risks his life and sacrifices a chance at love to protect a family of homesteaders from the corrupt, violent cattlemen who want to destroy them. *Shane* ends with a scene that has become part of Wild West mythology: the gunman rides off alone into the wilderness, bound for "some place I've never been." Watching him, yearning for him to return but knowing that he will not, is a young boy, a settler's son who has learned from the wanderer what it means to be a brave and honorable man. The hero Shane is a fictional creation, but his roots draw on both the reality and the mythology of the Wild West—that turbulent era of heroes, villains, and ordinary men and women living in an extraordinary time and place.

Carrying their goods in a Conestoga wagon, a pioneer family of the 1850s heads west along the National Road, a route that led from Maryland to Illinois, passing through the Ohio Valley. From the end of the National Road near the Mississippi River, other trails led farther west.

Chapter I

The Lure of the West

UNTIL THE 1860s, nearly all of those who lived, worked, and fought in the Wild West came from somewhere else. Even later, when the region had a permanent population that was giving birth to native-born westerners, people continued to stream into the West from other parts of the country and the world.

Why did they come? What drew them to a region that was, at first, beyond the boundary of the United States? Why would they move to a place where the landscape and weather were often harsh and unforgiving, where law and order were scarce? As with all human migrations, people came to the West for a wide variety of reasons. Many were escaping from trouble. For example, an immigrant named Johann Augustus Sutter fled his home country of Switzerland because he was deeply in debt. With grants of land from the Mexican government, he established a settlement near the site of present-day Sacramento. Sutter's Fort, as it was called, became a center of American activity in the area. A large group of immigrants fled to a different part of the West to escape from another kind of trouble—religious persecution. They were the Mormons, members of a newly founded religion, and they had been driven out of several midwestern states before establishing their own colony in Utah.

Many people were drawn to the West by the hope of economic improvement. Thousands dreamed of striking it rich in the gold or silver rushes. A few did, and many more set themselves up in business by providing the miners with food, supplies, and services such as lodging and laundry. But not everyone who came west saw the future as silver or gold. Some saw it as green: crops growing on the land they hoped to clear, homestead, and farm. For most who traveled to the West in the nineteenth century, supporting their families on their own farms or ranches was the goal.

Chinese miners in Colorado. Between 1849 and 1870, about 63,000 Chinese came to the United States, mostly to the West. Some eventually returned to China, but others stayed, forming the roots of Chinese-American communities.

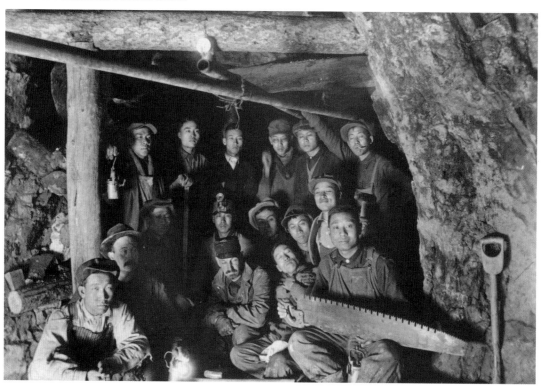

Some of those who populated the Wild West came there to find work. Among these were the Chinese immigrants who labored in the mines, built the western railroads, and founded Chinese-American communities across the West. Others came to fight—many of the U.S. Army troops who were posted to the West during the Mexican War or the later Indian wars settled in the region after leaving military service.

Finally, some of those who came to the West were driven by curiosity, restlessness, and the desire to see new places and have adventures. One of these was a boy named Charles M. Russell. In 1879 Russell lived with his family in Saint Louis, Missouri, where he read everything he could find about the wilder lands to the west. A talented artist, Russell filled a sketchbook with drawings of western scenes and characters, including one labeled "Buffalo Bill The American Scout." The following year, when Russell turned sixteen, his parents let him visit a family friend in Montana, where he accompanied a hunter named Jake Hoover on a wilderness expedition. As Russell later wrote, "To me, a boy lately from the east, riding by Jake's side through country like this seemed like a chapter from one of my favorite romances of the Rocky Mountains." Like other travelers before him, Russell had fallen under the spell of the West and would spend the rest of his life there.

The Mormons Look Westward: Joseph Smith's Diary

In 1830 a rural New Yorker named Joseph Smith founded a new sect called the Church of Jesus Christ of Latter-Day Saints,

Joseph Smith (*right*, shown here with his brother Hyrum) founded a new religion and hoped that his followers would be able to create an independent nation in the western wilderness.

also known as the Mormons. In the years that followed, Smith and the people he led established themselves in Ohio, Missouri, and finally Illinois. Mormon beliefs and practices—especially the custom of men having multiple wives—outraged many non-Mormons, and in 1844 an Illinois mob murdered him and his brother. Before his death, Smith had announced that the Mormons would seek a place to call their own, outside the laws of the United States and away from other communities. This diary entry, written a few months before his death, sets out Smith's hopes for a Mormon homeland.

"I instructed the Twelve Apostles to . . . investigate the locations of California and Oregon."

I INSTRUCTED THE TWELVE APOSTLES to send out a delegation, and investigate the locations of California and Oregon, and hunt out a good location where we can remove to after the Temple is completed, and where we can build a city in a day, and have a government

The Mormons' first community in Utah was Salt Lake City, seen here as it appeared in 1853, six years after settlement began. Industrious and well organized, the Mormons succeeded in planting productive farms and tidy towns in the barren landscape.

of our own, get up into the mountains, where the devil cannot dig us out, and live in a healthy climate where we can live as long as we have mind to.

—Diary of Joseph Smith, February 20, 1844. Reprinted in William Alexander Linn,
The Story of the Mormons. *New York: Macmillan, 1923.*

THINK ABOUT THIS

1. What qualities, according to Smith, made a "good location" for a Mormon settlement?
2. Smith mentions several goals for his followers in their new western home. Which do you think he would have considered most important?

"Everyone Is Going and No One Is Coming Back"

In January of 1848, a carpenter named James Marshall was building a sawmill for his employer, Johann Augustus Sutter. Marshall was working on the South Fork of the American River, in the foothills of the mighty Sierra Nevada range, when he found several pieces of bright, soft metal lying on the streambed. He had discovered gold, and although Sutter tried to keep the discovery secret, word soon leaked out. Throughout the summer of 1848, Californians swarmed into the hills to sift the streambeds for gold dust and nuggets. That fall, prospectors from Oregon, Mexico, and South America arrived, and during the winter, newspaper articles across North America and around the world set off what the *New York Herald* called "gold mania." By the following spring, tens of thousands of people, caught up in the frenzy, were heading toward the goldfields. Those who made it would become known as

Prospecting for gold seemed like a dashing, adventurous way to win a fortune. Most prospectors found only hard work, rough conditions, and disappointment.

the Forty-Niners. One of them wrote these words in his journal in Missouri, as he prepared to set out for California.

THIS OVERLAND JOURNEY is one of the most unfortunate undertakings to which man may allow himself to be lured, because he cannot possibly have any conception before starting of this kind of travelling. To be sure, there is a beaten path which you see clearly before you, but there are no stopping-places with even the slightest signs of civilization. Everyone is going and no one is coming back. You leave your camp in the hope of finding water, and a grazing place for the cattle a few miles further on; but sometimes it happens that you are forced to halt in a place where neither grass nor water can be found. This means intense suffering for the cattle and often an irretrievable loss.

"This overland journey is one of the most unfortunate undertakings."

—Hermann B. Scharmann, Overland Journey to California.
Freeport, NY: Books for Libraries Press, 1969. Originally published in 1918.

THINK ABOUT THIS

1. What do you think Scharmann meant by an irretrievable, or unrecoverable, loss?
2. Scharmann wrote these ominous words at the *beginning* of his trip westward, yet he continued the journey. Why do you think he did so?

Women Travel a Hard Road: Three Diaries

Women as well as men followed the wagon trails west during the mid-nineteenth century. Some of them came eagerly, drawn by the same forces that attracted men to the frontier: economic need, curiosity, restlessness, or the hope of making a fresh start. Most, however, came as the wives or daughters of men who had decided to relocate their families to the goldfields, new towns, or unsettled territories of the West. Many of these women recorded their experiences and thoughts about the journey and their new western homes in letters or diaries. These primary source documents, preserved by families or local historical societies, offer a glimpse of the challenges that women faced as they entered the Wild West.

THE TENTS DO NOT protect one from . . . winds—We were out of the range of Buffalo today, no game of any kind [. We passed] beyond the land of flowers too almost except the Cactus which is just beginning to bloom and is very beautiful—We met a party of "Arapahoes" today they approached us rather timidly at first were quite sociable afterwards & had a long talk which they carried on by signs. . . . When we were ready to start the Drum was beaten unexpectedly—& Indians and horses took to their heels pretty much frightened until they found it was only the signal for our departure [Anna Maria De Morris, June 15, 1850, on the Santa Fe Trail]

Still detained here on acct of rain. It rained incessantly all last night & this morning. It looks very gloomy. When it stops for a few moments the mountains seems to smoke. There are campt near us the 10 Californians. They have been there one year, made a fortune & glad to get back home. They say some 200 miles this side of there they found men without food eating their horses & mewls [mules]. One young man rather than eat his horse plunged in the river & drowned himself. There are also with the Californians men from Fort Larimee [Laramie] in search of deserters this season. Still rains & cold as winter. [Lucena Parsons, August 19, 1850, on the Oregon Trail]

> "One young man rather than eat his horse plunged in the river & drowned himself."

[T]his morning is vary clear and bright this day we have traveled seventeen miles to day noon we had the best grass I ever saw it looked like a perfect wheete field we then went on a little ways and come to the river their we found a man that had bin killed buy the Indians and his heart taken out he was buried yesterday and their lay a dead Indian it appears he was alone and the Indians came upon him and he shot one an then they shot him he was found with four arrows shot in his breast and the Indian found shot under one arm [Sarah Davis, September 19, 1850]

—In Kenneth L. Holmes, editor, Covered Wagon Women: Diaries and Letters from the Western Trails. Glendale, CA: Arthur H. Clarke, 1983.

THINK ABOUT THIS

1. Do these three women's experiences on the overland trails seem to have anything in common?
2. What kinds of information did the women think important to record in their journals?
3. How would you describe the tone of each diary entry? How do you think the women felt about their journey west?

"The Great West": A Senator Sees the Future

In 1850, Stephen A. Douglas was a senator from Illinois. When the Senate debated how to organize the new territory gained from Mexico under the Treaty of Guadalupe Hidalgo, Douglas delivered a speech that showed his passionate interest in the settlement of the West. A few years later, Douglas would write the Kansas-Nebraska Act of 1854, a controversial law that allowed settlers in the Great Plains territories—where an earlier agreement had banned slavery—to decide for themselves whether to allow slavery or forbid it. Although Douglas hoped that the act would prevent a split between the antislavery North and the proslavery South, in the end it only added to the conflict between the two sides that would soon erupt in the Civil War. Here is a portion of Douglas's speech to the Senate in 1850.

THERE IS A POWER in this nation greater than either the North or the South—a growing, increasing, swelling power, that will be able to speak the law to the nation. . . . That power is the country known as the great West—the Valley of the Mississippi, one and indivisible from the gulf to the great lakes, and stretching, on the one side and the other, to the extreme sources of the Ohio and the Missouri—from the Alleghenies to the Rocky mountains. There, sir, is the hope of this nation—the resting-place of the power that is not only to control, but to save, the Union? . . . This is the mission of the great Mississippi valley, the heart and soul of the nation and the continent.

—Stephen A. Douglas, speech to the Senate on March 13, 1850, in John C. Rives, editor, The Congressional Globe, Vol. XXL, Part 1. Washington, DC: John C. Rives, 1850.

1. How did Douglas define the West in geographic terms? Does his definition of the West differ from the modern one? If so, how?

2. In what way might Douglas have thought that the Mississippi Valley would "save" the Union?

"Pikes Peak or Bust": A New Gold Rush

In 1858, ten years after the discovery of gold at Sutter's Mill in California had kicked off the California gold rush, a mining expedition in the Colorado Rockies found gold near the mountain known as Pikes Peak after explorer Zebulon Pike. In the spring of the following year, thousands of hopeful prospectors descended on the region. Their slogan, sometimes painted on the sides of their wagons, was "Pikes Peak or Bust." Most of them busted. Only a handful of

Miners on their way to Pikes Peak, pictured in *Frank Leslie's Illustrated Newspaper* in 1859. This popular paper was one of the country's main sources of information—and misinformation—about the Wild West.

individual fortunes came out of the Pikes Peak gold rush. While the rush lasted, though, it fired people with feverish excitement, as this article from a Saint Louis newspaper shows (the spelling *Pike's* with an apostrophe would be considered an error today).

THOSE TWO LITTLE WORDS, "Pike's Peak," are everywhere. The latest [news] from Pike's Peak is eagerly devoured, no matter what it is. The quickest, safest route to Pike's Peak is what thousands want to know. Pike's Peak is in everyone's mouth and thoughts, and Pike's Peak figures in a million dreams. Every clothing store is a depot for outfits for Pike's Peak. There are Pike's Peak hats, and Pike's Peak guns, Pike's Peak boots, Pike's Peak shovels, and Pike's Peak goodness-knows-what-all, designed expressly for the use of emigrants and miners, and earnestly recommended to those contemplating a journey to the gold regions of Pike's Peak. We presume there are, or will be, Pike's Peak pills, manufactured with exclusive reference to the diseases of Cherry valley, and sold in conjunction with Pike's Peak guide books; or Pike's Peak schnapps to give tone to the stomachs of overtasked gold diggers; or Pike's Peak goggles to keep the gold dust out of the eyes of the fortune hunters; or Pike's Peak steelyards (drawing fifty pounds) with which to weight the massive chunks of gold quarried out of Mother Earth's prolific bowels. . . .

"Pike's Peak is in everyone's mouth and thoughts, and Pike's Peak figures in a million dreams."

steelyard
type of balance used for weighing objects

—Missouri Republican, *March 10, 1859, in Sanford Wexler, editor,* Westward Expansion: An Eyewitness History. *New York: Facts On File, 1991.*

1. What is the tone of this article? Does it give you a clue to the writer's opinion of the gold rush and the prospectors?
2. How does the marketing of Pikes Peak described in the article compare with modern marketing and advertising?

A Land of Wanderers: Horace Greeley's View of the West

Journalist Horace Greeley founded a newspaper called the *New York Tribune* and helped to establish the Republican Party. In his speeches and writings, he encouraged Americans to settle the western frontier and urged the government to make free land available to those who did so. Greeley investigated the West for himself in 1859 and, after returning to his home in the East, published a book about his experiences and impressions. In this passage, Greeley discusses a phenomenon that many visitors to the American

Newspaperman Horace Greeley was a major promoter of western settlement. When he ran for president in 1872, illustrator Thomas Nast ridiculed him in cartoons like this one and helped bring about his defeat.

West noticed—the fact that the West drew immigrants from every direction.

THE FIRST CIRCUMSTANCE that strikes a stranger traversing this wild country is the vagrant instincts and habits of the great majority of its denizens—perhaps I should say, of the American people generally as exhibited here. Among any ten whom you successively meet, there will be natives of New England, New York, Pennsylvania, Virginia or Georgia, Ohio or Indiana, Kentucky or Missouri, France, Germany, and perhaps Ireland. But, worse than this; you cannot enter a circle of a dozen persons of whom at least three will not have spent some time in California, two or three will have made claims and built cabins in Kansas or Nebraska, and at least one spent a year or two in Texas. Boston, New York, Philadelphia, New Orleans, St. Louis, Cincinnati, have all contributed their quota toward peopling the new gold region. The next man you meet driving an ox-team, and white as a miller with dust, is probably an ex-banker or doctor, a broken merchant or manufacturer from the old states, who has scraped together the candle-ends charitably or contemptuously allowed him by his creditors on settlement, and risked them on a last desperate cast of the dice by coming hither.

"The next man you meet driving an ox-team . . . is probably an ex-banker or doctor, a broken merchant or manufacturer from the old states."

candle-ends
leftover pieces, worthless scraps

—Horace Greeley, An Overland Journey from New York to San Francisco, in the Summer of 1859. *New York: Saxton, Barker & Co., 1860.*

1. What reasons does Greeley give to explain why people from all over might have come to the West?

2. Does this passage give you an idea of how Greeley felt about the people he met in the West?

"Orphans Preferred": The Pony Express

One of the biggest challenges for people in the Old West was the slow pace of communication. Mail took weeks to travel by ship between the east and west coasts of the country. The journey

A Pony Express rider waves at the workers who will soon put him out of work—the men who are putting up poles for the nation's first transcontinental telegraph line.

overland, by wagon or stagecoach, was faster, but not by much. In 1860, the Central Overland Express, a freight company that ran a stagecoach line across the West, launched a fast new mail service. Riders on swift horses, carrying up to fifteen pounds of mail in locked saddlebags, galloped from relay station to relay station between Saint Joseph, Missouri, and San Francisco, California. The Pony Express, as it was called, could carry a letter across the two thousand miles in ten to fourteen days. Less than two years later, a much cheaper and faster means of communication—the telegraph—put the Pony Express out of business. During its short life, the Pony Express had attracted about 180 footloose, adventure-seeking young men to work as riders. The first item here is an advertisement for riders. The second comes from William F. "Buffalo Bill" Cody's description of his brief service as a Pony Express rider.

*"WANTED:
Young skinny wiry
fellows..."*

WANTED: YOUNG SKINNY WIRY FELLOWS not over 18. Must be expert riders willing to risk death daily. Orphans preferred. WAGES $25 per week. Apply, Central Overland Express, Alta Bldg., Montgomery St.

—Advertisement for riders that appeared in Saint Louis and other cities. Reprinted in Glen D. Bradley, The Story of the Pony Express. Chicago: A. C. McClurg, 1920.

IN STRETCHING MY OWN ROUTE I found myself getting further and further west. Finally I was riding well into the foothills of the Rockies.

Still further west my route was pushed. Soon I rode from Red Buttes to Sweetwater [Wyoming], a distance of sixty-seven miles. Road-agents and Indians infested the country. I never was quite sure when I started out when I should reach my destination, or whether I should ever reach it at all.

road-agent
bandit

—*William B. Cody,* The Life of Honorable William F. Cody, Known as Buffalo Bill, the Famous Hunter, Scout, and Guide: An Autobiography. *Hartford, CT: Frank Bliss, 1879.*

THINK ABOUT THIS

1. Why do you think the Pony Express company wanted "skinny wiry" riders? And why might it have preferred orphans as employees?

2. What experiences as a Pony Express rider does "Buffalo Bill" Cody emphasize? What reason might he have for making these statements?

Chapter 2

The War Against the Native Americans

THROUGH THE STORY of the Wild West runs a dark and bloodstained theme: conflict between the first Americans and those who came later. True, people from many Native American groups enjoyed peaceful, even friendly, relationships with non-Indians. The larger picture, though, was one of violence on both sides. The Indians fought to hold on to the lands where they had lived for centuries, while the settlers, believing that they had the right and the need to use those lands, struggled for control of them. Some fights were skirmishes or raids that pitted settlers or trappers against small bands of Native Americans. Later, especially toward the end of the nineteenth century, the U.S. Army did much of the fighting against larger Indian forces.

The Indian Wars of the Wild West were the final phase of a conflict that had begun almost as soon as Christopher Columbus first landed in North America in 1492. Over the long course of that conflict, diseases brought to North America by the Europeans killed far more Native Americans than swords or bullets did,

Frederic Remington, *Cavalrymen in an Arizona Sandstorm.* Oil on canvas, 1889.

Cavalrymen in an Arizona Sandstorm, by Frederic Remington. In paintings, drawings, and sculptures, Remington (1861–1909) created hundreds of images of the West. Among his favorite subjects were Native Americans and U.S. soldiers—two groups that often, tragically, made war on one another in the final decades of the western frontier.

although it was the battles that people remembered. Gradually, as settlers moved west from the Atlantic coast, the native peoples either perished or migrated west themselves, away from the advancing line of settlement.

In 1830, the U.S. Congress tried to solve the "Indian problem" with the Indian Removal Act, which authorized the government to move Native Americans onto reservations—by force, if necessary. Indian nations living east of the Mississippi River had to relocate to present-day Oklahoma. To the north, the land across the Platte River remained in the hands of the Great Plains Indians. The United States government promised that those lands would remain the property of the Indians "for as long as the grass grows and the rivers run." But it seems that the grass soon stopped growing, and the rivers went dry. Wherever settlement increased, fighting broke out between whites and Indians: in the Pacific Northwest, in the southwestern territory newly acquired from Mexico, and in California. Before long conflict was raging in the Great Plains as well.

In the long run, the Indian Wars could end only one way. Although the Indians won some notable victories, they were greatly outnumbered. They could not withstand an organized, armed military assault forever. By the 1890s, they had been overpowered. Then, through laws that regulated such things as land ownership and Indian rights, the U.S. government tried to stamp out tribal identity and culture—to bring about what one federal official in 1887 called "the beginning of the end of the Indian as an Indian." The government did not succeed . . . not entirely. Native American culture survived in various forms, but by the end of the nineteenth century, the Native Americans were no longer a power in the land.

Throughout the Wild West era, the majority of Americans feared the Indians and wanted them controlled, perhaps even eliminated, although some citizens were deeply critical of the government's policies and acts toward the native peoples.

In the Cheyenne Country, John Hauser, 1896. Hauser (1859–1918) spent twenty years touring Native American reservations in the West and painting their inhabitants. Adopted by the Sioux nation in 1901, Hauser was given the Indian name Straight White Shield.

Toward the end of the era, however, triumph at the settlers' victory was tinged with shame, sadness, and a touch of nostalgia. To many people, the twilight of the Indian meant the end of the picturesque, traditional Old West. An artist named John Hauser captured that feeling in a 1902 painting called *Wild Horse*. It shows a Native American man who wears traditional Indian clothing, but he holds a rifle and his horse wears a European-style saddle. At his feet lies the sun-bleached skull of a buffalo—an animal, once the livelihood of the Plains Indians, that had been all but wiped out by white hunters. The painting's symbolism is clear: the old ways are dead or dying. Eleven years later the U.S. Mint issued a nickel with an Indian's head on one side and a buffalo on the other. Like Hauser's painting, the coin commemorated a world that Americans had hastened to destroy, yet mourned when it was gone.

Smallpox in the Dakotas

Of all the diseases that came to North America from Europe, historians agree that smallpox was the most destructive. Although it was dangerous to both Indians and non-Indians, it hit the Native Americans harder. Unlike people of European and African descent, Native Americans had not built up resistance to the disease during centuries of exposure. When an epidemic of smallpox swept through Indian communities or territories, the results were devastating—and settlers who escaped the disease risked being killed by Indians who blamed them for it. In 1837, a Philadelphia-born trader named Francis Auguste Chardon witnessed the effects of smallpox at Fort Clark in North Dakota, among Indians of the Mandan, Gros Ventre, and Arikara (Chardon called them Rees) nations. He recorded the events in his journal.

JULY 14
A young Mandan died to day of the Small Pox—several others has caught it—the Indians all being out Makeing dried Meat has saved several of them.

JULY 28

. . . This day was very Near to being my last—a young Mandan came to the Fort with his gun cocked, and secreted under his robe, with the intention of Killing me. After hunting me in 3 or 4 of the houses he at last found me. The door being shut, he waited some time for me to come out. Just as I was in the act of going out, Mitchel caught him, and gave him in the hands of two Indians who conducted him to the Village. Had not Mitchel perceived him the instant he did, I would not be at the trouble of Makeing this statement—I am upon my guard. . . . The Mandans & Rees gave us two splendid dances. They say dance, on account of their Not haveing a long time to live, as they expect to all die of the small pox—and as long as they are alive, they will take it out in dancing.

Men of the Mandan nation in the Dakotas perform a ritual called the Bison Dance in this 1844 engraving. Artworks such as this, created early in the settlement of the West, now provide valuable clues about Native American culture in the days before European influence.

JULY 30

Another report from the Gros Ventres to day say that they are arrived at their Village, and that 10 or 15 of them have died, two big fish among them. They threaten Death and Destruction to us all at this place, saying that I was the cause of the small pox Makeing its appearance in this country.

AUGUST 17

The Rees started out for buffaloe, the Indians dying off every day. Where the disease will stop, I know not. We are badly situated, as we are threatened to be Murdered by the Indians every instant; however we are all determined, and prepared for the worst.

"Where the disease will stop, I know not."

AUGUST 31

A young Mandan that died 4 days ago, his wife haveing the disease also, killed her two children, one a fine Boy of eight years, and the other six. To complete the affair she hung herself. The Number of Deaths up to the Present is very near five hundred—the Mandans are all cut off, except 23 young and Old Men.

SEPTEMBER 22

My youngest son died today.

—*Chardon, Francis Auguste,* Chardon's Journal at Fort Clark,
Annie Heloise Abel, editor. Pierre, SD: n.p., 1932.

THINK ABOUT THIS

Do you think that the Indians were right to blame the arrival of disease on the whites? If so, how do you feel about their desire for revenge?

The Indians Leave Yosemite

The Yosemite Valley in California's Sierra Nevada range contains some of the most dramatic and beautiful scenery in North America. It was long the home of several Native American groups, but the first whites known to have entered it were a party of fur trappers led across the mountains by Joseph Reddeford Walker in 1834. Fourteen or fifteen years later, the California gold rush drew miners into the Sierra valleys, including Yosemite, where they clashed with the Indian inhabitants. By that time California had become part of the United States, and the Americans in California assembled a group called the Mariposa Battalion to clear the Indians out of the valley. One member of the battalion, a doctor and miner, later wrote

A Frederic Remington illustration of a fur trader at an Indian council. Fur trappers and traders sometimes spent years living among the Indians, and many of them married Indian women.

about his dealings with a chieftain named Tenieya in the Yosemite Valley in March of 1851.

WE SUDDENLY CAME in full view of the valley. . . . None but those who have visited this wonderful valley can even imagine the feelings with which I looked upon the view that was there presented. The grandeur of the scene was but softened by the haze that hung over the valley—light as gossamer—and by the clouds which partially dimmed the higher cliffs and mountains. An exalted sensation seemd to fill my whole being and I found myself in tears with emotion.

. . . In the morning our Indian guide brought word from Tenieya that the old chief refused to consider any plan which would involve leaving the valley, and our scouts were sent out with instructions to bring him in, alive if possible. . . . The first sight that greeted him as he entered the camp was the dead body of his favorite son, shot while he attempted to escape. . . . The following night, unobserved by us, the body disappeared.

. . . [T]he captain gave orders for us to commence the search for [Tenieya's] people. . . . [W]e at length wound around a mountain spur and saw . . . a most beautiful little lake, to which I later gave the name Tenieya. . . . The Yosemites discovered our approach too late for either concerted resistance or successful escape. . . . No show of resistance was offered us, nor did any escape. . . . All hopes of avoiding a treaty or preventing their transfer to the reservation appeared to be at once abandoned. "Where can we now go that the Americans will not follow us?" asked the young chief in charge

> "Where can we now go that the Americans will not follow us? . . . Where can we make our homes that you will not find us?"

of this particular band. "Where can we make our homes that you will not find us?"

. . . I waited for Tenieya to come up and told him that we had given his name to the lake and the river. At first he seemed unable to comprehend our purpose, repeating: "It already has a name." Upon telling him that we had named it Tenieya because it was on the shores of the lake that we had found his people, who would never return to it to live, his countenance fell, and he at once left us and rejoined his own family circle. His expression as he left us seemed to indicate that he thought the naming of the lake no equivalent for the loss of the territory.

—*Lafayette Houghton Bunnell,* Discovery of the Yosemite and the Indian War of 1851. *Chicago: Fleming H. Revell, 1880.*

THINK ABOUT THIS

1. Compare Bunnell's "exalted" feelings on entering the valley with the actions that follow.
2. How would you describe Bunnell's conversation with Tenieya about the lake's new name? What do you think Bunnell's motives were? Was Tenieya's reaction reasonable?

Colonel Chivington and the Sand Creek Massacre

One of the most violent episodes of the Indian Wars took place in eastern Colorado after some Arapaho and Cheyenne Indians refused to move to a reservation. The Civil War was under way, and no federal troops could be spared to deal with the Indian unrest. The territorial governor authorized several groups of militia,

Minister and militia leader John Chivington went down in history as the cause of one of the bloodiest incidents in the history of relations between whites and Native Americans.

or volunteer soldiers, to defend white settlements. Colonel John Chivington, a minister, was one of the militia commanders. He led his force of about a thousand men against a camp of seven hundred Cheyenne. The Indians and their leader, Black Hawk, who believed that he had arranged peace terms with an officer at a nearby fort, were completely unprepared for Chivington's ruthless assault. Although the Cheyenne tried to surrender, the militia slaughtered several hundred of them, including women and children. Documents later published by the federal government cast light on Chivington and on the bloody events at Sand Creek on November 29, 1864.

THE CHEYENNES will have to be soundly whipped before they will be quiet. If any of them are caught in your vicinity, kill them as that is the only way.

—Order issued by Colonel John Chivington, May 31, 1864, in United States War Department, The War of Rebellion: A Compilation of the Official Records of the Union and Confederate Armies. Washington, DC: Government Printing Office, 1880–1891.

IN REGARD TO THESE INDIAN DIFFICULTIES, I think if great caution is not exercised on our part that there will be a bloody war. It should be our policy to try and conciliate them, guard our mails and trains well to prevent theft, and stop these scouting parties that are roaming over the country who do not know one tribe from another, and who will kill anything in the shape of an Indian. It will require but few murders on the part of our troops to unite all these warlike tribes of the plains. . . .

—Report by Major T. McKinney, June 15, 1864, in United States
War Department, The War of Rebellion: A Compilation of the Official
Records of the Union and Confederate Armies. *Washington, DC:*
Government Printing Office, 1880–1891.

AS TO COLONEL CHIVINGTON, your committee can hardly find fitting terms to describe his conduct. Wearing the uniform of the United States, which should be the emblem of justice and humanity; holding the important position of commander of a military district, and therefore having the honor of the government to that extent in his keeping, he deliberately planned and executed a foul and dastardly massacre which would have disgraced the worst savage among those who were the victims of his cruelty.

—Report of the Committee on the Conduct of War, U.S. House
of Representatives, 1865, in Stan Hoig, The Sand Creek Massacre.
Norman: University of Oklahoma Press, 1961.

THINK ABOUT THIS

1. Does Chivington's approach to relations with the Native Americans seem appropriate for a minister?
2. What does the wording of the final entry tell about attitudes toward Indians in the 1860s, even on the part of those who condemned Chivington's acts?

Corruption on the Reservation: A Sioux Man's Testimony

The federal government appointed agents to manage the Indian reservations and distribute the supplies provided by the government for the Native Americans who lived on them. Some of these Indian agents did their job well, but many did not. They stole supplies intended for the Indians and sold them for their own profit, and they also profited from shady deals involving reservation land or resources. After the Civil War ended in 1865, Congress investigated the state of affairs on Indian reservations. Its report included testimony from a Yankton Sioux man named Struck by the Ree, who lived in the Dakota Territory.

THE FIRST AGENT WAS REDFIELD; and when he came there he borrowed blankets from me to sleep upon, and agreed to return them, but never did, though I asked for them. Goods have been stored up stairs in the warehouse, and have all disappeared; perhaps the rats ate them; I don't know what became of them. If they bring any goods for the Indians to eat and put them in the warehouse, the agents live out of them, and the mess-house where travellers stop has been supplied from the Indians' goods, and pay has been taken by the agents, and they have put the money in their pockets and taken it away with them. I have seen them take the goods from the storehouse of the Indians and take them to the mess-house, and I have had to pay for

> *"If they bring any goods for the Indians to eat and put them in the warehouse, the agents live out of them."*

Sioux men and women line up to receive government food supplies at Pine Ridge, one of the reservations onto which western Indians were forced in the late nineteenth century. The federal government's plan was to turn the Native Americans of the Great Plains from roving hunters into settled farmers, although farming was completely foreign to their culture and experience.

a meal for myself at the mess-house, and so have others of our Indians had to pay for meals at the mess-house, prepared from their own goods.

—*In* Condition of the Indian Tribes, *Senate Report 156, 39th Congress, 2nd session. Washington, DC: Government Printing Office, 1867.*

THINK ABOUT THIS

1. If Struck by the Ree's account is true, how had agent Redfield cheated the Indians in his care?
2. Can you think of any reasons agent Redfield might have offered to justify stealing from the Indians?

A Different Kind of War: Assimilation

When the fighting ended, what was the U.S. government going to do with the Indians? The answer was a new policy called assimilation. The government wanted Native Americans to become assimilated, or absorbed, into the larger American culture. Whether or not they lived on reservations, Indians were to be encouraged—or, in some cases, forced—to live as much like other Americans as possible. Overseeing this process was the Bureau of Indian Affairs. In his official 1885 report, the head of the bureau described the goal of assimilation.

"... they must forsake their savage habits and learn the arts of civilization."

EVERY STEP TAKEN, every move made, every suggestion offered, everything done with reference to the Indians should be with a view of impressing upon them that this is the policy which had been permanently determined upon by the Government in reference to their management. They must abandon tribal relations; they must give up their superstition; they must forsake their savage habits and learn the arts of civilization; they must learn to labor, and must learn to rear their families as white people do, and to know more of their obligations to the Government and to society.

—*John Atkins, Commissioner of Indian Affairs, in J. P. Kinney,*
A Continent Lost—A Civilization Won. *Baltimore: Johns Hopkins Press, 1937.*

1. What do you think Atkins meant by the "arts of civilization"?
2. How would you compare the policy of assimilation that Atkins described in 1885 with American attitudes and practices toward other cultures today?

"If Peace Is Possible We Will Have It"

The last big battle of the Indian Wars took place at the end of 1890. Four years earlier, General Nelson Miles had accepted the surrender of the Apache chieftain Geronimo in Arizona. Now he was

LEFT: General Nelson Miles was victorious at Wounded Knee Creek, the last major Indian battle. BELOW: After Chief Big Foot perished at Wounded Knee, the army photographed his body as proof of his death.

supposed to bring order to South Dakota, where many Sioux had joined a religious and political movement, the Ghost Dance, that called for the Indians to regain control of the region. Less than a month after Miles sent the following message to army headquarters in Washington, DC, three hundred Sioux and twenty-five army soldiers died at the Battle of Wounded Knee Creek.

". . . they will prefer to die fighting rather than starve peaceably."

subsistence
minimum of food necessary for survival

THE INDIANS ARE BETTER ARMED NOW than they ever were and their supply of horses is all that could be desired. Every buck has a Winchester rifle, and he knows how to use it. In the matter of subsistence they are taking little risk. They can live on cattle just as well as they used to on buffalo, and the numerous horse ranches will furnish them with fresh stock, when cold and starvation ruin their mounts. The Northern Indian is hardy and can suffer a great deal. These hostiles have been starved into fighting, and they will prefer to die fighting rather than starve peaceably.

I hope the problem may be solved without bloodshed, but such a happy ending to the trouble seems impossible. An outbreak would cost the lives of a great many brave men, and the destruction of hundreds of homes. . . . If peace is possible we will have it.

—*Message from General Nelson Miles, December 1, 1890, in James P. Boyd,* Recent Indian Wars. *Philadelphia: Franklin News Company, 1891.*

1. Do you think Miles believed that peace with the Sioux was possible?

2. What advantages did the Indians have heading into battle? Why do you think those advantages were not enough to bring them victory over Miles's troops?

Frank Tenney Johnson (1874–1939) spent part of his life in the West and became a well-known illustrator of western scenes. *The Deputy Sheriff* is one of his many images of cowboys under the stars. In these pictures, the artist developed a style that came to be known as the "Johnson moonlight technique."

Violence and Justice on the Frontier

FOR YEARS, POPULAR BOOKS, movies, and television shows have portrayed the Wild West as a violent place where six-guns blazed daily, Indians or bandits attacked every stagecoach, no bank was safe from robbers, and mobs of angry people calling themselves vigilantes were ever ready to take the law into their own hands. At the same time, however, historians have debated just how violent the West really was, and whether the image of Western violence has helped shape modern American culture.

Roger D. McGrath of the University of California conducted one of the most detailed studies of Old West violence and reported his findings in *Gunfighters, Highwaymen & Vigilantes: Violence on the Frontier* (1984). McGrath sifted through primary sources: the newspapers of two Sierra Nevada mining towns—Aurora in western Nevada and Bodie in eastern California—from the 1860s through the 1880s. He collected information on the number and type of crimes that had been reported, and the results paint a picture that is a bit different from the widely held image of Wild West violence. No banks were robbed. Juvenile crime, rape, and racial violence were nonexistent. Typical crimes were burglaries and robberies of individuals or stagecoaches. Warfare between Indians and whites—chiefly the ranchers who were moving into the area—was another source of violence. The most common crime, however, was gunfighting among miners and the rough, sometimes criminal characters that people called "badmen." The badmen were not the only ones to go armed—most male citizens, and some female ones, carried guns and were ready to defend themselves and their property. They did not carry them in holsters, as so often seen in movies and on television, but usually in a pocket or resting in a waistband.

McGrath's research convinced him that, as he wrote, "some long-cherished notions about violence, lawlessness, and justice in the Old West—especially those created by movies and, still worse, television—are nothing more than myths." Many other historians share his conclusion. Still, all agree that patterns of crime differed from place to place and time to time in the Old West. Violence, in various forms and sometimes deadly, was a fact of life for many people. Some observers of modern culture believe that the legacy of Wild West violence, part reality and part mythology, has influenced such aspects of modern life as gun ownership and the use of fighting and other violence in games and entertainment.

"Bleeding Kansas": Two Views of Fighting on the Frontier

Before Kansas became a state in 1861, it was a frontier territory. The Kansas-Nebraska Act of 1854 gave settlers the right to vote on

In an 1856 illustration, proslavery Missourians head west to burn and loot Lawrence, Kansas, whose citizens opposed slavery. "Bleeding Kansas" was part of a larger picture of frontier conflict.

whether or not to allow slavery in the territory. When elections took place the following year, about 6,000 people cast votes—despite the fact that the population of the Kansas Territory at the time was only about 1,500. Most of the other votes were cast by the "border ruffi-ans," proslavery Missourians who had crossed the border to swing the election. They elected a proslavery government for the territory, but antislavery settlers refused to accept it and elected their own government. Conflict between the two sides was so violent that the territory became known as "Bleeding Kansas." As the following offi-cial government communications show, however, slavery was not the only source of conflict. The first selection is from a letter from the governor of the Kansas Territory to the U.S. secretary of state; the second comes from a letter sent by a federal official in Kansas to a new governor. Together they reveal a territory in turmoil.

ONE OF THE GREATEST, if not the greatest, obstacle to overcome in the production of peace and harmony in the territory, is the unsettled condition of the claims to the public lands. These lands are very considerably covered by settlers, many of whom have expended much labor and money in the improvement of their claims, to which, as yet, they have no legal title. These improved claims have excited the cupidity of lawless men; many of whom, under the pretense of being actuated by either anti-slavery or pro-slavery proclivities, drive off the settlers and take possession of their property. The persons thus driven off, having no legal title to their claims, have no redress at the hands of the law, and in many instances have patiently and quietly submitted to their wrongs, and left the country: while others, and still a greater portion, have retreated to the towns, combined together, and prepared themselves to defend and maintain what they justly conceive to be their rights, by meeting violence with violence.

—*Governor John W. Geary, Kansas Territory, to Secretary of State William L. Marcy, September 22, 1856, in Murlin G. Welch,* Border Warfare in Southeast Kansas, 1856–1859. *Pleasanton, KS: Linn County Publishers, 1977.*

"Our town is filled with armed men."

I WRITE IN THE MIDST OF REVOLUTION—Our town is filled with armed men—For several weeks our town has been threatened with conflagration & pillage—This morning we were awakened with the cry that the enemy were upon us, and such was the fact—A large body of armed men came into our town, just at day-break, and declared their intention to lay the town in ashes, unless certain individuals who, from their political opinions, had become obnoxious to them, were delivered into their custody—

—*U.S. land office employee Epaphroditus Ranson to Governor James W. Dorner, Kansas Territory, February 11, 1858, in Murlin G. Welch,* Border Warfare in Southeast Kansas, 1856–1859. *Pleasanton, KS: Linn County Publishers, 1977.*

THINK ABOUT THIS

1. According to Governor Geary, what are the motives for the attacks on settlers?

2. When reading the second source, can you tell what the "obnoxious" political opinions were? Does it matter?

3. How far should people go in dealing with those with whom they disagree?

Vigilantism: Citizens as Executioners

The rough-and-ready, independent spirit of the Wild West extended to ideas about law and order. When a crime occurred away from the reach of established law enforcement, members of the community might deal with the guilty party themselves. The crowds that served out frontier justice weren't always unruly mobs. Often citizens organized themselves into semi-military units called Committees of Vigilance, from which the terms *vigilantism* and *vigilantes* come. They might simply drive those they considered guilty out of town, but they did conduct executions, usually by hanging but occasionally

A hanging by vigilantes in Colorado in the 1880s. In areas where official law enforcement was stretched to its limit—or beyond it—citizens sometimes took matters into their own hands. The large crowd is a reminder that many people regarded executions as public entertainment.

by shooting. As time went on, vigilantism became more than a substitute for nonexistent law enforcement. Even in places that had marshals, sheriffs, judges, or other authorities, people might take the law into their own hands if they felt that the sheriff had not done his job properly, or if they disagreed with a judge's handling of a case or a jury's verdict. Sometimes vigilantism preserved order and protected the community; all too often, however, it was just another form of lawlessness. The following primary sources give two views of frontier vigilantism. The first is a petition or plea to the governor of the Nevada Territory from a group of concerned residents. The second is a newspaper article about a vigilante hanging.

YOUR PETITIONERS, RESIDENTS AND CITIZENS of Aurora, Esmeralda County, Territory of Nevada would most respectfully represent: That there is now an armed organization in our midst, acting in open defiance of the law and constituted authorities; that this organization, without even the pretence of legal right, is continuing to arrest citizens and residents among us, and compelling them, by an overwhelming force, to leave and abandon a place where they have seen fit to come and live. These proceedings are being carried on by an armed multitude, overpowering the legally constituted officers, upon the pretext of charges that are **preferred** in secret against parties protesting their entire innocence, and who are denied the opportunity of defence, or confronting their accusers, or even of knowing who they are.

preferred
brought up

. . . We, therefore, your petitioners, earnestly urge upon your excellency to adopt some measures by which our society may be held and protected within the law, the imminent danger of a disastrous outbreak and bloodshed be avoided, and the rights of all be protected and secured.

—*People of Aurora, March 3, 1864, in Hubert Howe Bancroft,* Popular Tribunals
(1887). Reprinted in Roger D. McGrath, Gunfighters, Highwaymen & Vigilantes:
Violence on the Frontier. *Berkeley: University of California Press, 1984.*

THE SUMMARY HANGING at Bodie of the Frenchman DaRoche by the Vigilantes of that reckless camp will probably have the effect of checking if not crushing out the spirit of lawlessness which has so long terrified its people. When the officers of the law persistently fail to do their duty, and the courts, established for the promotion of justice, prove themselves unequal to the task, it is time for the people to rise in their majesty and vindicate the first great law of self-preservation. . . . Deplore, as we may, that condition of society which requires the gathering of a mob to execute the decrees of justice, it is an improvement over

summary
*without
formality*

that other high state of civilization which allows murder to run riot in a community and allows assassins to walk the streets unharmed.

—*Virginia City, Nevada,* Territorial Enterprise, *January 20, 1881.*
Reprinted in Roger D. McGrath, Gunfighters, Highwaymen & Vigilantes: Violence on the Frontier. *Berkeley: University of California Press, 1984.*

THINK ABOUT THIS

1. How do these two sources differ in their views of vigilantism?

2. Do you think that one makes a better case than the other? Which one?

Two Tough Towns: Wichita and Dodge City

Kansas had some of the wildest towns in the Wild West—until citizens grew tired of what one local newspaper discreetly called "rowdyism." The cattle trails from Texas ended at "cow towns" such as Wichita and Dodge City, where dealers bought and sold thousands of head of cattle while cowboys spent their wages in saloons, gambling dens, and other places of entertainment. This mixture of big business and long-awaited pleasure made the cow towns exciting places, sometimes explosive ones. A sign outside Wichita asked visitors to "Leave

William Barclay "Bat" Masterson combined two western professions: gambler and lawman. He served briefly as a sheriff in Kansas and a marshal in Colorado.

Wichita, Kansas, as it appeared in 1874. Drawings such as this one are informative but perhaps not completely reliable.

This primary source photograph shows the lawmen of Dodge City, Kansas, in the late 1870s: (*seated, left to right*) Charlie Bassett, Wyatt Earp, M. F. McLean, and Neal Brown, and (*standing, left to right*) W. H. Harris, Luke Short, Bat Masterson, and W. Petillon.

your revolvers at police headquarters," but brawls were common and gunfights occasionally erupted; the cow towns had to hire lawmen such as Wyatt Earp and Bartholomew "Bat" Masterson to keep order. These descriptions of the two towns come from an 1872 Kansas newspaper article and a book by a man who lived in Dodge City in the 1870s.

THE POPULATION OF WICHITA is decidely heterogeneous. Here may be seen people of every class, shade and character. The sleek and well dressed speculator, with airs suggestive of genteel living and plethoric purses; the independent, money-making, money-spending, somewhat don't-care-a-cuss-ativeness cattle drover; the rollicking, reckless, free-and-easy herder; the substantial citizen; the professional gambler, and the long-haired desperado of the plains, are here brought together of necessity.

—*Topeka, Kansas,* Daily Commonwealth, *October 15, 1872, in Sanford Wexler, editor,* Westward Expansion: An Eyewitness History. *New York: Facts On File, 1991.*

"... the cowboy came because it was his duty as well as his delight; ... the gambler and the bad man came because of the wealth and excitement."

SOME CAME TO DODGE CITY out of curiosity; others strictly for business; the stockman came because it was a great cattle market, and here, in the Arkansas river, was the place appointed for the cattle going north to be classed and passed on, for bargains to be closed, and new contracts made for next year; the cowboy came because it was his duty as well as his delight, and here he drew his wages and spent them; the hunter came because it was the very heart of the greatest game country on earth; the freighter came because it was one of the greatest overland freight depots in the United States, and he hauled material and supplies for nearly four hundred miles, supplying three military posts, and all the frontier for that far south and west; last but not least, the gambler and the bad man came because of the wealth and excitement, for obscene birds will always gather around a carcass.

—*Robert M. Wright,* Dodge City: The Cowboy Capital.
Wichita: Wichita Eagle Press, 1913.

THINK ABOUT THIS

1. What do Wichita and Dodge City have in common in these two descriptions?
2. What elements of a typical community do *not* appear in these descriptions?

Diary of a Range War

Cattle ranching caused many Old West conflicts. At first, ranchers could simply round up herds of the wild or half-wild descendants of Spanish cattle that roamed the plains. Mavericks, as these cattle were called, were most numerous in Texas, but their range spread into the Great Plains as the range of the buffalo shrank. In time, cattlemen began branding herds and laying claim to streams and grazing territory on publicly owned land. They also began illegally fencing tracts of these public lands. Clashes erupted over "fence cutting," the removal of illegal fences by other ranchers. Other conflicts pitted small, independent ranchers and homesteaders against the growing might of the big cattle companies. In Wyoming

William H. D. Koerner's 1928 painting *Rustlers* captures the pell-mell pace of cattle stealing on the frontier. On the rangelands of the West, rustling livestock was a serious crime.

in the 1890s, the Wyoming Stock Growers Association claimed control of all unbranded mavericks. Small ranchers who dared to defy the big cattle interests were accused of "rustling," or cattle stealing (some may have been rustlers, but many were not). In 1892, fifty-two armed men called the Regulators—cattlemen and hired thugs—came to Johnson County, along the Powder River, to deal out their own brand of justice to the small ranchers they called rustlers. A settler named Nate Champion was besieged in his cabin by the Regulators. He recorded their attack as it happened, in the form of a diary for his friends. Finally, the Regulators set fire to Champion's cabin. When he fled the flames, they shot and killed him.

. . . THEY ARE STILL SHOOTING and are all around the house. Boys, there is bullets coming in like hail. Them fellows is in such shape I can't get at them. They are shooting from the stable and river and back of the house.

Boys, I feel pretty lonesome just now. I wish there was someone here with me so we could watch all sides at once. They may fool around until I get a good shot before they leave. . . . There was a man in a buckboard and one on horseback just passed. They [the attackers] fired on them as they went by. I don't know if they killed them or not. . . .

"Boys, there is bullets coming in like hail."

I shot at the men in the stable just now; don't know if I got any or not. I must go and look out again. It don't look as if there is much show of my getting away. I see twelve or fifteen men. . . . They are shooting at the house now. . . . Well, they have just got through shelling the house like hell. I heard them splitting wood. I guess they are going to fire the house tonight. I think I will make a break when night comes, if alive. It's not night yet.

The house is all fired. Good-bye, boys, if I never see you again.

—*Diary of Nate Champion, April 9, 1892, printed in the* Cheyenne, Wyoming, Daily Leader, *April 13–20, 1892. Reprinted in Wayne Gard,* Frontier Justice. *Norman: University of Oklahoma Press, 1949.*

THINK ABOUT THIS

1. What is your opinion of the Regulators' actions?
2. Do you think it matters whether or not Champion was a rustler?
3. How might the Johnson County War have been avoided?

Chapter 4

Cattle and Cowboys

SOME OF THE MOST ENDURING images of the Wild West concern the cowboy. Cowboys did not own the herds of cattle that they tended—the owners were known as stockmen or cattlemen (or women). But the actual work of branding cattle, rounding them up, and getting them to market was done by hired laborers: the cowboys.

The first cowboys were the vaqueros, Mexican horsemen who tended cattle herds on the dry northern plains of Mexico. Americans in Texas adopted the vaqueros' methods and equipment, including the lasso and the protective leather leggings called chaps. As the cattle industry developed in the West, the image of the hardworking hired cattle herder developed along with it, until by the late 1870s the term *cowboy* had come into wide use.

Although people had long raised both beef cattle and dairy cows in the East, the western cattle industry was different. For one thing, much of the West was far dryer than the East. Pastures were less lush. The cattle best suited to Texas and the Plains territories

The cowboy's job was hard and often lonely. For years cowboys were seen as roughnecks and ruffians, but by the 1880s an image of the heroic, noble cowhand was taking shape.

were longhorns, lean, hardy cattle that could survive on tough, wiry grasses and brush.

The western cattle industry began in Texas before the Civil War. It was open-range ranching, in which the herds roamed freely over open land—this was possible in the West, where vast tracts of land were (and still are) owned by the government.

A vaquero, painted by Frederic Remington

Unlike the domestic cattle raised on farms and ranches in the East, western cattle were practically wild. They essentially raised themselves, seeking out food and water on their own until a crew of herders rounded them up and drove them to market in Missouri, Kansas, or Wyoming. These "long drives," as they were called, began in 1866, when herders drove about 200,000 longhorns out of Texas, and continued through the 1880s.

Cattle ranching in the West could be quite profitable because there was so little cost to the cattlemen, who did not have to pay for land, water, or feed for their animals. Within a few years, the herds had been largely branded and had passed into private ownership. Some owners were cattle barons who lived in the West, but many were easterners or even foreign companies—one of the biggest of these firms, the Prairie Cattle Company, controlled ranges from Colorado to Texas but belonged to investors in Scotland. In the 1880s, however, the oversupply of cattle caused a sharp drop in the price of beef and in ranchers' profits. At the same time, western weather struck three hard blows at the cattle industry: drought in Texas in 1884, severe winter weather in Texas and the Southwest in 1886, and, in 1887, a winter so brutal on the Plains that it killed at least a third of the cattle in Montana and Wyoming.

Open-range ranching and the long cattle drives soon faded into history. The cattle industry continued to be an important part of the western economy, but smaller herds grazed ranges that were likely to be fenced. Cowboys no longer made the historic cattle drives, but as ranch employees, full-time or seasonal, they continued to do a distinctively western job.

"The Country Is Alive with Stock": The Cattle Industry Takes Hold

The first important center of the western cattle industry was Texas. In 1865, when soldiers who had left Texas to fight in the Civil War returned to their home state, they found huge herds of longhorns roaming wild—as many as five million animals, historian Paul Robert Walker reports in *Trails of the Wild West* (1997). An item published in a New York paper that year showed how quickly the cattle industry was becoming established.

Cowboys moving a cattle herd, photographed in 1910 by Erwin E. Smith. As both cowboy and artist, Smith (1886–1947) wanted to make accurate, realistic records of cowboy life to stand against the romantic images of fiction and the movies.

A TEXAS LETTER WRITER SAYS: 'Any man in this State who does not own 400 head of cattle and 70 or 100 horses and mules is worse than worthless. . . . As far as the eye can reach in any direction, and as far as you may go the country is alive with stock. The whole markets of the United States might be supplied here, and there would not be any apparent decrease.'

—Frank Leslie's Illustrated Newspaper. *November 4, 1865.*

1. What effect do you think such newspaper items might have on an eastern reader?

2. Does the tone of the letter strike you as realistic or exaggerated? Why might the writer of the letter have chosen that tone?

Teddy Roosevelt Remembers the Great Die-Off of 1886

Theodore Roosevelt, a New Yorker who later became president, spent several years in the mid-1880s living and ranching in the Dakota Territory. The books he wrote about his experiences became immensely popular and helped form the public's early-twentieth-century ideas about the West and its people and ways of life.

Theodore Roosevelt on his Dakota ranch

ABOUT THE MIDDLE OF November the storms began. Day after day the snow came down, thawing and then freezing and piling itself higher and higher. By January the drifts had filled the ravines and coulées almost level. The snow lay in great masses on the plateaus and river bottoms; and this lasted until the end of February. The preceding summer we had been visited by a prolonged drought, so the scanty grass was already well cropped down; the snow covered what pasturage there was to a depth of several feet, and the cattle could not get at it at all, and could hardly move around. It was all but impossible to travel on horseback—except on a few well-beaten trails. It was dangerous to attempt to penetrate the Bad Lands, whose shape had been completely altered by the great white mounds and drifts. The starving cattle died by scores of thousands before their helpless owners' eyes. The bulls, the cows who were suckling calves, or who were heavy with calf, the weak cattle that had just been driven up on the trail, and the late calves suffered most; the old range animals did better, and the steers best of all; but the best was bad enough.

> *"The starving cattle died by scores of thousands before their helpless owners' eyes."*

—*Theodore Roosevelt,* Ranch Life and the Hunting Trail. *Lincoln: University of Nebraska Press, 1983. Originally published 1888.*

THINK ABOUT THIS

1. Based on this excerpt, what kind of people do you think Roosevelt would consider well suited to ranching in the West?

2. What does this passage suggest about the relationship between the natural environment and human economic activities?

The Cowboy as a Bad Guy: Sensational Papers Paint a Dark Picture

Many people outside the West got their ideas about cowboys and other Wild West figures from popular, inexpensive publications. One of the most influential was *Frank Leslie's Illustrated Newspaper,* which appeared in 1855 and continued to be published for forty years, although the name was changed to *Frank Leslie's Illustrated Weekly* for the final four. Its rival, also published in New York City, was the *Police Gazette.* Both papers drew heavily on stories and pictures of violence in the West. The villains were sometimes outlaws and sometimes cowboys— and sometimes there was little or no difference between the two.

In Without Knocking (1909), by Charles M. Russell, highlights the wilder side of cowboy behavior.

WHILE IN TOWN [the cowboy's] home is in the saloons and the dance houses. He soon gets gloriously drunk and then begins to yell like a wild Indian and shoots his big revolvers promiscuously into the crowd. He is little else than a crazy demon at such times and woe betide the man who crosses his path.

"He is little else than a crazy demon."

—*"The Cow-Boy of the Plains. A Sketch of a Very Boisterous and Often Murderous Character,"* Police Gazette, *September 6, 1879.*

WHEN "OFF-DUTY" COWBOYS are a terror in the way they manifest their exuberance of spirits. Two or three will dash through a town, and, before the people know what is going on, will have robbed every store of importance and made their escape.

—*"Texan Cowboys on a Holiday Excursion,"* Frank Leslie's Illustrated News, *January 14, 1881.*

THINK ABOUT THIS

1. Can you think of reasons why these papers' publishers might have been glad to print stories about crime or violence?
2. Do you see any similarities between these papers and some of today's publications?

The Cowboy as a Good Guy: The Image of a Frontier Hero Emerges

Starting in the mid-1880s, the cowboy portrayed in newspapers and magazines changed slowly from a ruffian to a noble fellow—a bit rough around the edges in terms of polish and style, but decent, brave, and honorable. What shifted the popular idea of the cowboy from villain to hero? Articles in literary magazines presented a more positive image of the western cattle herder, and so did some books, including Roosevelt's writings and the first cowboy autobiography, Charles A. Siringo's *A Texas Cowboy,* published in 1885. Also important was Buffalo Bill's Wild West Show, organized by William F. Cody, a former western scout, hunter, and soldier who had become famous as an actor and the hero of many adventure stories. His traveling show opened in 1883 and included "Cowboy Fun," a display of riding and bull roping by cowboys that proved very popular among the millions of people who saw the show in the United States and Europe. Less than a decade later, social historians Eleanor Marx and Edward Aveling credited Cody's show with transforming the image of the cowboy. Following are three commentaries on the new, "rehabilitated" cowboy.

"Altogether cow-boys are a whole-souled, large-hearted, generous class of fellows."

COW-BOYS AS A CLASS ARE brimful and running over with wit, merriment, good-humour. They are always ready for a bit of innocent fun, but are not perpetually spoiling for a fight, as has so often been said of them. . . . They have been known . . . to resort to acts of real abuse and injury against defence-less people. But such acts on the part of genuine cow-boys are rare, and are rigorously condemned by all the respectable element in the business. Altogether cow-boys are a whole-souled, large-hearted, generous class of fellows . . . and it is safe to say that nine-tenths of

A 1908 poster for "Buffalo Bill" Cody's Wild West show, a long-lasting and wildly popular traveling entertainment. The mustachioed Cody appears near the center front of the poster, holding his hat.

the hard things that have been said of them have come from men who never knew a single one of them.

—Harper's Weekly, *October 16, 1886.*

IN THIS CATTLE DRIVING BUSINESS is exhibited some of the most magnificent horsemanship, for the "cow-boys," as they are called, are invariably skillful and fearless horsemen—in fact only a most expert rider could be a cow-boy.

—*William F. Cody,* An Autobiography of Buffalo Bill.
New York: Cosmopolitan Publishers, 1923.

TO MOST PEOPLE, until lately, the cowboy was a "bold, bad man," as reckless of the lives of others as of his own, with vague values as to morals, and especially as to the rights of property; generally full of whiskey, and always handy with a revolver. If the spectators of the "shows" in which he has been exhibited on both sides of the Atlantic have modified their ideas upon this human subject, the modification has been . . . recognition of the fact that he is not much worse or better morally than his more civilised fellows, and in his manners, as in his physique, he is for the most part considerably the superior of these.

—*Eleanor Marx and Edward Aveling,* The Working-Class Movement in America. *London: Swann & Sonnenschieb Co., 1891.*

THINK ABOUT THIS

1. Does the *Harper's Weekly* image of the cowboy seem more or less convincing than that presented in the *Police Gazette*?

2. Why might Marx and Aveling have thought that the cowboy's manners and physique were better than those of most "civilised" people? Judging from this excerpt from their book, can you form any ideas about what kind of cowboys they might have met or seen?

"Big Swimming": A Cowboy's Recollections

In the early 1870s, during the heyday of the long, open-range cattle drives, James H. Cook signed on to help drive a herd of Texas cattle north to Kansas through the Indian Territory, as present-day Oklahoma was then called. Each of the three main trails—the Western, the Chisholm, and the Shawnee—crossed the Red

In a view of cowboy life that is less glamorous (but probably more authentic) than the Wild West show, two Arizona cowboys share the task of mending a piece of saddle gear while a third reads in the shade under their wagon. Erwin E. Smith photographed them in 1909.

River at the border between Texas and the Indian Territory. Farther north, they crossed the Arkansas River. Between those two watercourses, the cowboys encountered many smaller streams and rivers—but as Cook found on his first cattle drive, in some years these rivers weren't so small.

THIS FIRST YEAR THAT I was on the trail, every river from the Red River to the Arkansas was "big swimming," as the boys termed it. We were fortunate in having no serious accidents, but we lost a number of both cattle and horses by drowning. We had some bad hail- and thunder-storms. Sometimes we went for days at a stretch with scarcely a wink of sleep, because of winds and rain, which made the cattle hard to control. In some places on the trail the country would become very boggy after a long rainy spell, and we had

". . . we lost a number of both cattle and horses by drowning."

to resort to all sorts of schemes to snatch a little sleep when an opportunity presented itself. When three riders could get away at a time they would go a little way from the cattle and dismount, each man holding his horse by the bridle rein. Then they would lie down in the form of a triangle, each man using his neighbor's ankles for a pillow. In this manner the sleeper's heads were up out of the mud and water.

—*James H. Cook,* Fifty Years on the Old Frontier: As Cowboy, Hunter, Guide, Scout, and Ranchman. *New Haven: Yale University Press, 1923.*

THINK ABOUT THIS

Does Cook's account of cowboy life match images you may have from books, movies, or television? How is it the same or different?

Good guys and bad guys—which is which? The two sides of this confrontation
are not easy to identify. Real life in the West could be equally confusing.
Some individuals were outlaws at one time and lawmen at another.

Chapter 5

Outlaws and Lawmen

N O PART OF WILD WEST HISTORY has drawn more attention than tales of the outlaws who terrorized the West and the lawmen who hunted them down. And no part of western history is more packed with conflicting stories, contradictory sources, mythmaking, tall tales, and uncertainty. Although modern historians have done much to uncover the truth about these Wild West villains and heroes, in many cases the final truth can probably never be known.

Some of the confusion comes from the way stories have been retold and rewritten over the years by hundreds of journalists and writers, often for entertainment rather than scholarship. But part of the uncertainty comes from the primary sources themselves. Materials written at the time events happened, such as newspaper reports, were often based on statements passed along by witnesses, or by people who claimed to have spoken with witnesses. There is no way to check the accuracy of most such items. In some cases, though, the people involved wrote their own stories (or had them written by professional ghostwriters and then signed their names to them). The Texas badman John Wesley Hardin and the cow-town marshal Wyatt Earp, for example, are among many who left accounts of their exploits in their own words. Can't these be trusted? Not really. Not only is the true authorship of some of these accounts questionable, but people's memories do not always preserve details accurately. And people do not always tell the truth.

The outlaws and lawmen of the Old West—like many others who were part of that era—often exaggerated for the sake of telling a good story or to create a more powerful, memorable image of themselves. Sometimes they flat-out lied. By comparing multiple sources and carefully weighing the likely reliability of each, historians are arriving at a better understanding of who the outlaws and lawmen really were and what they really did. No amount of historical accuracy, however, can change the fascination that characters such as Billy the Kid, Jesse James, Doc Holliday, and Bat Masterson will continue to hold. If some of their deeds were a bit less spectacular than was once thought, they were still remarkable individuals whose boldness—on the side of the law or against it—made them the most colorful people in a very colorful era.

The Texas Ranger and the Fugitive: J. B. Gillett's Memoirs

Although settlers in Texas formed militia forces called "Rangers" as early as the 1820s, the well-known Texas Rangers of the Old West dated from 1874. That year the governor of Texas established the Frontier Battalion of the Texas Rangers, 450 men in six brigades that acted as a statewide police force under military-style

The original Texas Rangers were a loosely organized band of ranchers and farmers who tried to protect Texas from outlaws, Mexicans, and Indians. In 1840 John C. Hays (*front center*, in white shirtsleeves) joined this militia and improved its discipline and organization. Later in the century, the governor established a more professional force.

organization. J. B. Gillett joined the Rangers as a young man and spent the late 1870s fighting crime in Kimble County, the haunt of a number of badmen. One of them was Dick Dublin, wanted for murder. Gillett's memoir of his time as a Ranger describes his hunt for this fugitive.

ON THE EXTREME HEADWATERS of the South Llano River some cattlemen had built a large stock pen and were using it to confine wild cattle. This was far out beyond any settlement and probably fifty or sixty miles from our camp. I thought it possible that Dick Dublin might be hanging around the place, so we traveled through the wood most of the way to it. Here I found that the cattlemen had moved . . . so we began our return journey.

. . . On the fourth day I timed myself to reach the Potter ranch about night. Old man Potter, a friend and neighbor of Dublin's, lived here with two grown sons. It was known that Dublin frequented the place, and I hoped to catch him here unawares. . . .

We knew the moment we left the creek bed we would be in full view of the Potters and the ranch house. We decided, then, that we would advance on the house as fast as we could run. . . . We rose from the creek running. Old man Potter discovered us as we came into view and yelled, "Run, Dick, run! Here come the Rangers!"

"I ordered him to halt and surrender, but he had heard that call too many times and kept going."

We then knew that the man we wanted was at the camp. We were so close upon Dublin that he had no time to mount his horse or get his gun, so he made a run for the brush. I was within twenty-five yards of him when he came from behind the wagon, running as fast as a big man could. I ordered him to halt and surrender, but he had heard that call too many times and kept going. Holding my Winchester carbine in my right hand I fired a shot directly at him as I ran. In a moment he was out of sight.

I hurried to the place where he was last seen and spied him running up a little ravine. I stopped, drew a bead on him, and again ordered him to halt. As he ran, Dublin threw his hand back under his coat as though he were attempting to draw a pistol. I fired. My bullet struck the fugitive in the small of the back. . . . It killed him instantly.

—*James B. Gillett,* Six Years with the Texas Rangers, *1875–1881.*
Austin TX: Von Boeckmann-Jones, 1921.

THINK ABOUT THIS

1. How would you compare law enforcement in Gillett's day with the same job today?

2. Why do you think Gillett so carefully described Dublin's actions at the moment of the shooting?

The Death of Billy the Kid

Born in New York City in 1859, Henry McCarty had moved by the early 1870s to New Mexico, where he was called by the name of his stepfather, Billy Antrim. In later years he would also be known as William Bonney and Billy the Kid. He became a small-time thief and horse rustler, and in 1878, working for a group of local cattlemen, he took part in a range war in New Mexico's Lincoln County. When it ended, Billy the Kid was wanted for murder (popular legend said that Billy had killed more than twenty men, but the true number is probably four). Sheriff Pat Garrett captured Billy in 1880. Billy was sentenced to hang, but he escaped the noose by escaping from jail. In April of 1881, Garrett then tracked him to the home of a friend named Pete Maxwell. Garrett's autobiography, ghostwritten for the sheriff by a journalist named Ashmun Upson, gives an exciting account of the outlaw's final minutes.

Billy the Kid, in a photograph that has been painted

. . . IT WAS NEAR TO MIDNIGHT and Pete was in bed. I walked to the head of the bed and sat down on it, beside him, near the pillow. I asked him as to the whereabouts of the Kid. He said that the Kid had certainly been about, but he did not know whether he had left or not. At that moment a man sprang quickly into the door, looking back, and called twice in Spanish, "Who comes there?" No one replied and he came on in.

He was bareheaded. From his step I could perceive he was either barefooted or in his stocking-feet, and held a revolver in his right hand and a butcher knife in his left.

He came directly towards me. Before he reached the bed, I whispered: "Who is it, Pete?" but received no reply for a moment. . . .

"Quickly as possible I drew my revolver and fired, threw my body aside and fired again."

The intruder came close to me, leaned both hands on the bed, his right hand almost touching my knee, and asked, in a low tone:—"Who are they, Pete?"—at the same instant Maxwell whispered to me. "That's him!" Simultaneously the Kid . . . raised quickly his pistol . . . within a foot of my breast. Retreating rapidly across the room he cried: *"Quien es? Quien es?"* (Who's that? Who's that?) All this occurred in a moment. Quickly as possible I drew my revolver and fired, threw my body aside and fired again. The second shot was useless; the Kid fell dead. He never spoke. A struggle or two, a little strangling sound as he gasped for breath, and the Kid was one with his many victims.

—*Pat Garrett,* The Authentic Life of Billy the Kid. *Santa Fe: New Mexico Printing and Publishing Co., 1882.*

1. Do you think Pat Garrett's version of events is reliable? Why or why not?

2. What do you think of Maxwell's role in the matter?

Wyatt Earp and the OK Corral

One of the most famous shoot-outs in Wild West history took place on October 26, 1881, in Tombstone, Arizona, near the OK Corral. Four of the men were lawmen: the Earp brothers—Wyatt, Virgil, and Morgan—and their friend Doc Holliday. The other five—Tom and Frank McLaury, Ike and Billy Clanton, and Billy Clayton—were what Wyatt Earp called "hard men," possibly cattle rustlers. Some time earlier, Ike Clanton had agreed to give Wyatt Earp information about a stagecoach robbery in exchange for a reward. Then, apparently fearing that the robbers would kill him for betraying them, Clanton sent for friends to help him kill Earp and his fellow lawmen to prevent the arrangement from becoming known. Fifteen years after the showdown at the OK Corral, Earp authored an account of the event for a San Francisco newspaper. Western chronicler James D. Horan claims in *The Authentic Wild West: The Lawmen* (1980) that the piece was ghostwritten for Earp by someone on the paper's staff and is "filled with distortions, half-truths, and lies . . . the beginning of the Earp-manufactured legend." Still, Earp's thrilling version of events has become enshrined in western lore.

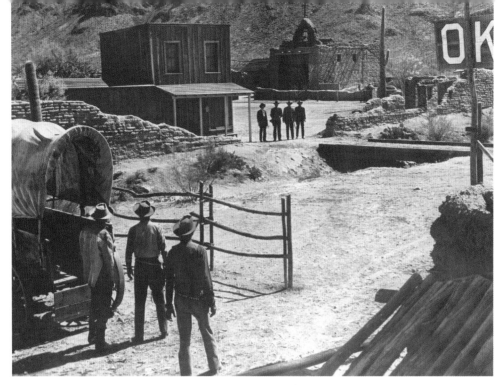

A scene from the 1957 film *Gunfight at the O.K. Corral*, directed by John Sturges. This and other films about the legendary showdown tend to follow Wyatt Earp's version of events, which may be largely fictional.

THEY CAME GALLOPING into town, loaded up with ammunition and swearing to kill us off in short order. Thirty or forty citizens offered us their help but we said we would manage the job alone.

"What had we better do?" Virgil asked.

"Go and arrest 'em," I said.

The four newcomers and Ike Clanton had stationed themselves on a fifteen-foot lot between two buildings . . . and sent word that if we did not come down and fight they would waylay and kill us. So we started down after them—Doc Holliday, Virgil, Morgan, and I. As we came to the lot they moved back and got their backs against one of the buildings.

"I'm going to arrest you boys," said Virgil.

For answer their six-guns began to spit. Frank McLaury fired at me and Billy Clanton at Morgan. Both missed. I had a gun in my overcoat pocket and I jerked it out at Frank McLaury, hitting him in the stomach. At the same time Morgan shot Billy Clanton in the breast. So far we had the best of it, but just then, Tom McLaury, who had got behind his horse fired under the animal's neck and bored a hole right through Morgan sideways. The bullet entered one shoulder and came out at the other.

"I got it, Wyatt," said Morgan.

"Then get behind me and keep quiet," I said—but he didn't.

By this time bullets were flying so fast I could not keep track of them. Frank McLaury had given a yell when I shot him and made for the street, one hand over his stomach. Ike Clanton and Billy Clayton were shooting fast and so was Virgil, and the two latter made a break for the street. I fired a shot which hit Tom McLaury's horse and made it break away, and Doc Holliday took the opportunity to pump a charge of buckshot out of a Wells Fargo shotgun into Tom who promptly fell dead. In the excitement of the moment, Doc Holliday didn't know what he had done and threw away the shotgun in disgust, pulling his six-shooter instead.

Then I witnessed a strange spectacle. Frank McLaury and Billy Clanton

". . . bullets were flying so fast I could not keep track of them."

Actor Burt Lancaster, playing Marshal Wyatt Earp, during the movie's gunfight scene were standing in the middle of the street, both badly wounded, emptying their six-shooters like lightning. One of them shot Virgil through the leg and he shot Billy Clanton. Then Frank McLaury started to his feet and staggered across the street, though he was full of bullets. On the way he came face to face with Doc Holliday.

"I got ye now, Doc," he said.

"Well, you're a good one if you have," said Holliday with a laugh.

With that they both aimed. But before you can understand what happened next I must carry the narrative back half a minute.

After the first exchange in the lot Billy Clanton had gotten into one of the buildings from the rear and when I reached the street he was shooting out of one of the front windows. Seeing him aim at Morgan I shouted: "Look out, Morg, you're getting it in the back!"

Morgan wheeled around and in doing so fell on his side. While in that position he caught sight of Doc Holliday and Frank McLaury aiming at each other. With a quick drop he shot McLaury in the head. At the same instant McLaury's pistol flashed and Doc Holliday was shot in the hip.

That ended the fight. . . . It may or may not surprise some readers to learn that from the first to the last shot fired, not more than a minute elapsed.

—"How Wyatt Earp Routed a Gang of Arizona Outlaws,"
San Francisco Examiner, *August 2, 1896.*

THINK ABOUT THIS

1. If you could interview Earp about this episode, what would you ask him?

2. Do you think that the Earps and Holliday made the right response to Clanton's threat? Can you think of other things they could have done?

The Wild Bunch Robs a Train

Among the last of the Wild West outlaws were a group of rustlers and robbers called the Wild Bunch (they were also known as the Hole in the Wall Gang). One of the group's leaders was Robert Leroy Parker, called Butch Cassidy. An outlaw named Harry Longabaugh, known as the Sundance Kid, helped Parker carry out several robberies of Union Pacific trains, which transported money as well as mail and passengers. One such robbery took place on June 2, 1899, near Wilcox, Wyoming. A mail clerk on the train wrote an eyewitness description for a local paper.

Under the name Butch Cassidy, a cattle thief and robber named Robert Leroy Parker became one of the last famous outlaws of the West.

AS SOON AS WE CAME TO A STANDSTILL, Conductor Storey went forward to see what was the matter and saw several men with guns, one of whom shouted that they were going to blow up the train with dynamite. The conductor understood the situation at once and, before meeting the bandits, turned and started back to warn the second section. The robbers mounted the engine and at the point of their guns forced the engineer and fireman to dismount, after beating the engineer over the head with their guns, claiming he didn't move fast enough, and marched them back over to our car.

. . . In about 15 minutes two shots were fired into the car, one of the balls passing through the water tank and on through the stanchions.

Following close upon the shooting came a terrific explosion, and one of the doors was completely wrecked and most of the car windows broken. The bandits then threatened to blow up the whole car if we didn't get out, so Bruce gave the word and we jumped down, and were immediately lined up and searched for weapons. They said it would not do us no good to make trouble, that they didn't want the mail—that they wanted what was in the express car and was going to have it, and that they had powder enough to blow the whole train off the track.

. . . The robbers then went after the safes in the express car with dynamite and soon succeeded in getting into them, but not before the car was torn to pieces by the force of the

"The bandits then threatened to blow up the whole car if we didn't get out."

Harry Longabaugh, also known as the Sundance Kid, teamed with Parker for several train and bank robberies. Although the two are thought to have been killed in South America around 1908, it was rumored that at least one of them returned to the United States in disguise.

charges. They took everything from the safes and what they didn't carry away they destroyed. After finishing their work they started out in a northerly direction on foot.

. . . The men all wore long masks reaching below their necks and of the three I observed, one looked to be six feet tall, the others being about ordinary sized men. The leader appeared to be about 50 years old and spoke with a squeaky voice, pitched very high.

They appeared not to want to hurt anyone and were quite sociable and asked one of the boys for a chew of tobacco. . . .

—*Robert Lawson, "Butch Cassidy and the Sundance Kid Rob the Union Pacific," Buffalo, Wyoming,* Bulletin, *June 8, 1899. Reprinted in Larry Pointer,* In Search of Butch Cassidy. *Norman: University of Oklahoma Press, 1977.*

THINK ABOUT THIS

1. Does Lawson give any clues as to how he felt about the attack?
2. What image of the robbers is given by this account?
3. The victim of the robbery was a railroad company. What effect do you think this might have had on how people viewed the crime?

No. 54   THE ARTHUR WESTBROOK CO.
Cleveland, Ohio   Vol. V

DENVER DOLL WAVED HER TORCH TO AND FRO ABOVE HER HEAD, AND SCREAMED AT THE TOP OF
HER VOICE, FRANTIC WITH FEAR THAT NO HEED WOULD BE TAKEN OF HER.

Part of the Deadwood Dick Library of dime-novel publisher Beadle and Adams, the story *Denver Doll as Detective* managed to combine two popular types of tale: the detective story and the western. Thousands of inexpensive books like this one fed the public's hunger for colorful adventures set in the Wild West.

Chapter 6

Entertainment, Literature, and Myth

CHARLES M. RUSSELL, the boy artist from Saint Louis who went to Montana in 1880, fell in love with the place and made it his home for many years. He became a well-known artist who tried to capture, in his paintings and illustrations, the wild, free, frontier spirit that had shaped his boyhood dreams of the West. As he grew older, Russell realized that the Wild West, the Old West, was disappearing: "trails plowed under," he called it. By that time, however, the Wild West was becoming a familiar subject in many different kinds of popular art and entertainment—including Russell's own paintings.

One new form of entertainment that appeared in the mid-nineteenth century did a lot to promote the image of the Wild West. It was the dime novel—a short, inexpensive paperback book aimed at young people and working-class readers. Between 1860 and 1900, the four main publishers of dime novels, all based in New York City, issued about ten thousand titles. Perhaps as many as half of them dealt with western adventure. Hundreds of them concerned William F. "Buffalo Bill" Cody alone. Others starred real western personalities such as Kit Carson or Calamity Jane, but with little concern for historical accuracy.

Even before becoming a character in dime novels, Buffalo Bill had acted in stage plays based on his adventures—or his alleged adventures. In 1883 he launched a third form of entertainment—his Wild West show, which featured an Indian attack on a stagecoach, a buffalo hunt, a horse race, a rodeo, and exhibitions of trick shooting and riding. The show toured North America and Europe for decades. Writer Mark Twain, who had spent some time in the West and written his own account of it in *Roughing It* (1872), saw Cody's show and declared, "Down to its smallest details, the show is genuine, cowboys, vaqueros, Indians, stage coach, costumes and all." Cody colored people's ideas about the West for several generations.

The West became the subject of a different kind of show in 1898, when Thomas Edison, inventor of the movie camera, made the first two western films: silent pictures called *Cripple Creek Bar Room Scene* and *Poker at Dawson City,* both just a few minutes long. Edwin S. Porter's ten-minute *The Great Train Robbery* (1903) was one of the most successful early films and set the pattern for many, many more movies to come: good guys and bad guys in a shoot-out. Starting in 1915, actor William S. Hart became famous by starring in a long string of western movies. Other heroes on horseback followed, and for years the western remained a major category of movies and, later, television.

Why was the Wild West so popular? At least part of the answer lies in the social and economic developments that transformed the United States as the nineteenth century drew to a close and

Although it was filmed in New Jersey, the 1903 movie *The Great Train Robbery* created a tremendous appetite for western films. It included a scene of a bandit firing his gun directly at the camera. Because movies were still very new to most people, many terrified audience members thought they really were about to be shot.

the twentieth began. The country was well on its way to being a predominantly industrial, urban nation. As the frontier life of the West waned, people became nostalgic for it. They came to see it as a simpler, better time that represented values that many liked to think were especially American: toughness, individualism, and independence.

Nowhere does the nostalgia for the Old West come across more clearly than in the cowboy paintings of Frederic Remington and the writings of his friend, novelist Owen Wister. Both men were very much aware that they were marketing a vanishing Old West in their work. In 1900 Remington wrote to Wister, "As you know I am working on a big picture book—of the West and I want you to write a preface . . . telling the . . . public that this is the real thing—step up and buy a copy—last chance—ain't going to be any more west etc." Two years later, Wister published his own ode to the vanished West: a novel called *The Virginian,* the story of a rough but noble westerner, an eastern schoolteacher, and an epic gunfight illustrating the "code of the West." So popular was this best seller that when Wister and his family visited the West in 1911, a number of people claimed that the Virginian must have been based on a real-life person known to them. Wister's wife recognized the mythmaking power of the book when she remarked, "It was written as fiction but has become history."

The Dime Novel: *Deadwood Dick's Doom*

The dime novels were hastily written, and few of them hold much literary merit. But they appealed to readers' taste for adventure and escape from the everyday world. Most dime novels were melodramas, a type of storytelling that is deliberately not realistic, with exaggerated emotions, colorful and dangerous plot events, and larger-than-life characters who represent extremes of good and evil.

In this scene from *Deadwood Dick's Doom,* for example, a saloonful of rough characters in a wicked town called Death Notch react to a new arrival.

FEW THERE WERE in Death Notch who had not heard of the notorious girl, and several among the lot had seen, and now recognized her, Poker Jack among the rest, for Poker had formerly thrived in Deadwood, before taking in Pioche and Death Notch.

Calamity had changed but little since the time when this pen last introduced her: she was the same graceful, pretty girl-in-breeches that she had always been, but if there was any change it was in the sterner expression of her sad eyes.

"A murmur of 'Calamity Jane,' ran through the bar-room as she entered."

A murmur of "Calamity Jane," ran through the bar-room as she entered, proving that she was recognized by more than one.

"Yes Calamity Jane!" she retorted. "I see I am not unknown even in this strange place. Better perhaps, is it so, for you'll have a clearer idea of whom you have to deal with. I want to know where Deadwood Dick is, that's what I want. I allow ye'll say he ain't here, but I won't swallow that. He told me he'd be here, over a week ago, an' he allus keeps his dates."

"An' so you are wantin' him, eh?" Piute Dave grunted, from his perch on one end of the bar. "S'pose likely you're a pard o' his'n eh?"

"I allow I've been his truest pard for many a year," Calamity replied, "but that's not what I was asking. Where is Deadwood Dick?"

"Well, gal, ef my memory serves me right, I allow the last I see'd o' him he was a-sinkin' in a bed of quicksand, where I throwed him.

We had a tassel, an' ther best man was ter chuck t'other 'un in the quicksand, an' ther honor fell onto me. He weakened and I give him a boost, an' I presume ef he's kept right on sinkin' ever since he's arriv' down ter ther maiden kentry o' the washee washee, by this time."

Calamity's heart sunk within her at this declaration but outwardly she was very calm.

She had [seen] Deadwood Dick in the lower mining districts, a few weeks before, and he had said, as he took her hand in his, in parting:

"I'm going up to Death Notch, Janie, on my last adventuresome trail, and after that I'm going to settle down for good, in some lonely spot and see if the remainder of my life cannot be passed in more peace and quiet than the past has been. Come to me at Death Notch, Calamity, and the hand you have so long sought shall be yours. We will go hence down the avenue of life, hand in hand together as man and wife."

And then he had kissed her good-by, and she had looked forward eagerly for the appointed time to come when she should go to claim the love and protection of the only man she had ever worshipped.

—*Edward L. Wheeler,* Deadwood Dick's Doom; or, Calamity Jane's Last Adventure. *New York: Beadle and Adams, ca. 1899.*

THINK ABOUT THIS

1. From the way Dave, Jane, and Dick talk, does it seem likely that they occupy the same social class or come from the same background? Whose way of speaking seems most likely to be realistic? Least likely?

2. Based on this scene, can you guess what is going to happen next?

3. Is there any doubt as to who the "good guys" and "bad guys" of the story are?

"Please Do Not Shoot the Pianist": Oscar Wilde's West

Travelers from Europe occasionally toured the American West and then wrote about their adventures. In 1882, as part of a lecture tour, the Irish writer Oscar Wilde visited the gold- and silver-mining town of Leadville, Colorado. Here Wilde claims to have delivered a lecture to the miners of Leadville on the works of the sixteenth-century Italian goldsmith Benvenuto Cellini.

FROM SALT LAKE CITY one travels over the great plains of Colorado and up the Rocky Mountains, on the top of which is Leadville, the richest city in the world. It has also got the reputation of being the roughest, and every man carries a revolver. I was told that if I went there they would be sure to shoot me or my traveling manager. I wrote and told them that nothing they could do to my traveling manager would intimidate me.

"They were miners—men working in metals—so I lectured to them on the Ethics of Art."

They were miners—men working in metals—so I lectured to them on the Ethics of Art. I read them passages from the autobiography of Benvenuto Cellini and they seemed much delighted. I was reproved by my hearers for not having brought him with me. I explained that he had been dead for some little time, which elicited the enquiry, "Who shot him?"

reproved
criticized

They afterwards took me to a dancing saloon where I saw the only rational method of art criticism I have ever come across. Over the piano was printed a notice:

Please Do Not Shoot the Pianist.
He Is Doing His Best.

The mining boomtown of Leadville, Colorado, as it appeared in *Frank Leslie's Illustrated Newspaper* in 1879, three years before Oscar Wilde's visit.

The mortality among pianists in this place is marvelous.

Then they asked me to supper, and having accepted, I had to descend a mine in a rickety bucket in which it was impossible to be graceful. Having got into the heart of the mountain I had supper, the first course being whiskey, the second whiskey and the third whiskey.

I went to the Theatre to lecture and I was informed that just before I went there two men had been seized for committing murder, and in that theatre they had been brought onto the stage at eight o'clock in the evening and then and there tried and executed before a crowded audience. But I found these miners very charming and not at all rough.

—*Oscar Wilde,* The Complete Writings of Oscar Wilde. *Vol. 9,*
Impressions of America. *New York: Pearson, 1909.*

1. When decribing the people and places of the West, what tone does Wilde use?
2. What do you think was Wilde's purpose in writing this passage? Who might his intended readers have been?

The Virginian: Model of a Western Hero

In this excerpt from Owen Wister's *The Virginian*, a newcomer from the East surveys a western town and witnesses a confrontation between the novel's protagonist, the black-haired Virginian, and a fellow named Trampas.

TOWN, AS THEY CALLED IT, pleased me the less, the longer I saw it. But until our language stretches itself and takes in a new word of closer fit, town will have to do for the name of such a place as was Medicine Bow. I have seen and slept in many like it since. Scattered wide, they littered the frontier from the Columbia to the Rio Grande, from the Missouri to the Sierras. They lay stark, dotted over a planet of treeless dust, like soiled packs of cards. Each was similar to the next, as one old five-spot of clubs resembles another. Houses, empty bottles, and garbage, they were forever of the same shapeless pattern. More forlorn they were than stale bones. They seemed to have been strewn there by the wind and to be waiting till the wind should come again and blow them away. Yet serene above their foulness swam a pure and quiet light, such as the East never sees; they might be bathing in the air of creation's first morning. Beneath sun and stars their days and nights were immaculate and wonderful.

Medicine Bow was my first, and I took its dimensions, twenty-nine buildings in all,—one coal shute, one water tank, the station, one store, two eating-houses, one billiard hall, two tool-houses, one feed stable, and twelve others that for one reason and another I shall not name. Yet this wretched husk of squalor spent thought upon appearances; many houses in it wore a false front to seem as if they were two stories high. There they stood, rearing their pitiful masquerade amid a fringe of old tin cans, while at their very doors began a world of crystal light, a land without end, a space across which Noah and Adam might come straight from Genesis. Into that space went wandering a road, over a hill and down out of sight, and up again smaller in the distance, and down once more, and up once more, straining the eyes, and so away.

· · ·

Five or six players sat over in the corner at a round table where counters were piled. Their eyes were close upon their cards, and one seemed to be dealing a card at a time to each, with pauses and betting between. Steve was there and the Virginian; the others were new faces.

"No place for amatures," repeated the voice; and now I saw that it was the dealer's. There was in his countenance the same ugliness that his words conveyed.

"Who's that talkin'?" said one of the men near me, in a low voice.

"Trampas."

"What's he?"

"Cow-puncher, bronco-buster, tin-horn, most anything."

"Who's he talkin' at?"

"Think it's the black-headed guy he's talking at."

"That ain't supposed to be safe, is it?"

"Guess we're all goin' to find out in a few minutes."

"Been trouble between 'em?"

"They've not met before. Trampas don't enjoy losin' to a stranger."

Novelist Owen Wister in 1900. The Philadelphia-born, Harvard-educated Wister, who attended a European boarding school and became a lawyer, was "the unlikeliest of creators for his celebrated book," says *Harvard Magazine*, adding, "A cowboy he wasn't." But Wister did spend fifteen summers on western ranches, observing and writing, before creating *The Virginian*.

"Fello's from Arizona, yu' say?"

"No. Virginia. He's recently back from havin' a look at Arizona. Went down there last year for a change. Works for the Sunk Creek outfit."

•   •   •

. . . There had been silence over in the corner; but now the man Trampas spoke again.

"AND ten," said he, sliding out some chips from before him. Very strange it was to hear him, how he contrived to make those words a personal taunt. The Virginian was looking at his cards. He might have been deaf.

"AND twenty," said the next player, easily.

The next threw his cards down.

It was now the Virginian's turn to bet, or leave the game, and he did not speak at once.

Therefore Trampas spoke. "Your bet, you son-of-a—."

The Virginian's pistol came out, and his hand lay on the table, holding it unaimed. And with a voice as gentle as ever, the voice that sounded almost like a caress, but drawling a very little more than usual, so that there was almost a space between each word, he issued his orders to the man Trampas: "When you call me that, SMILE." And he looked at Trampas across the table.

Yes, the voice was gentle. But in my ears it seemed as if somewhere the bell of death was ringing; and silence, like a stroke, fell on the large room. All the men present, as if by some magnetic current, had become aware of this crisis. In my ignorance, and the total stoppage of my thoughts, I stood stock-still, and noticed various people crouching, or shifting their positions.

"Sit quiet," said [one of them], scornfully to the man near me. "Can't you see he don't want to push trouble? He has handed Trampas the choice to back down or draw his steel."

"...with a voice as gentle as ever, ...he issued his orders to the man Trampas: 'When you call me that, SMILE.'"

At least five movies and one television series have been made of *The Virginian* since 1914. This scene is from the 1946 film, starring Joel McCrea.

Then, with equal suddenness and ease, the room came out of its strangeness. Voices and cards, the click of chips, the puff of tobacco, glasses lifted to drink,—this level of smooth relaxation hinted no more plainly of what lay beneath than does the surface tell the depth of the sea.

For Trampas had made his choice. And that choice was not to "draw his steel." If it was knowledge that he sought, he had found it, and no mistake! We heard no further reference to what he had been pleased to style "amatures." In no company would the black-headed man who had visited Arizona be rated a novice at the cool art of self-preservation.

—*Owen Wister,* The Virginian: A Horseman of the Plains. *New York: Macmillan, 1902.*

THINK ABOUT THIS

1. What qualities does Wister give to his setting in his opening description? Does anything in this description suggest what might be the themes of the coming story?
2. How is the Virginian different from the people around him? What values does he represent?

Mary Austin's *The Land of Little Rain*

Gunfights and showdowns were not the only subjects for authors drawn to the West. Mary Austin, who grew up in Illinois but spent much of her later life in southern California, was a pioneer of another kind of western writing. Her books focused on the land and its unique creatures, terrain, and natural rhythms of life. Austin incorporated people's stories into her books as well, but her greatest strength as a writer lay in describing the landscape and its effect on those who lived in it. She was one of the first to celebrate the nature of the West in print.

EAST AWAY FROM THE SIERRAS, south from Panamint and Amargosa, east and south many an uncounted mile, is the Country of Lost Borders.

Ute, Paiute, Mojave, and Shoshone inhabit its frontiers, and as far into the heart of it as a man dare go. Not the law, but the land sets the limit. Desert is the name it wears upon the maps, but the Indian's is the better word. Desert is a loose term to indicate land that supports no man; whether the land can be bitted and broken to that purpose is not proven. Void of life it never is, however dry the air and villainous the soil.

This is the nature of that country. There are hills, rounded, blunt, burned, squeezed up out of chaos, chrome and vermilion painted, aspiring to the snowline. Between the hills lie high level-looking plains full of intolerable sun glare, or narrow valleys drowned in a blue haze. The hill surface is streaked with ash drift and black, unweathered lava flows. After rains water accumulates in the hollows of small closed valleys, and, evaporating, leaves hard dry levels of pure desertness that get the local name of dry

Mary Austin (1868–1934) helped pioneer a new style of western writing based on personal experience and love of the land. *The Land of Little Rain* led the way for modern western nature writers such as Wallace Stegner.

lakes. Where the mountains are steep and the rains heavy, the pool is never quite dry, but dark and bitter, rimmed about with the efflorescence of alkaline deposits. A thin crust of it lies along the marsh over the vegetating area, which has neither beauty nor freshness. In the broad wastes open to the wind the sand drifts in hummocks about the stubby shrubs, and between them the soil shows saline traces. The sculpture of the hills here is more wind than water work, though the quick storms do sometimes scar them past many a year's redeeming. In all the Western desert edges there are essays in miniature at the famed, terrible Grand Cañon, to which, if you keep on long enough in this country, you will come at last.

"The sculpture of the hills here is more wind than water work."

Since this is a hill country one expects to find springs, but not to depend upon them; for when found they are often brackish and unwholesome, or maddening, slow dribbles in a thirsty soil. Here you find the hot sink of Death Valley, or high rolling districts where the air has always a tang of frost. Here are the long heavy winds and breathless calms on the tilted mesas where dust devils dance, whirling up into a wide, pale sky. Here you have no rain when all the earth cries for it, or quick downpours called cloud-bursts for violence. A land of lost rivers, with little in it to love; yet a land that once visited must be come back to inevitably. If it were not so there would be little told of it.

—*Mary Austin,* The Land of Little Rain. *Boston: Houghton Mifflin, 1903.*

THINK ABOUT THIS

1. How would you explain Austin's affection for the landscape she describes?

2. Why might Austin emphasize the inhospitable nature of this landscape?

Zane Grey, Mythmaker

Ohio-born Zane Grey became famous for his tales of the western frontier. He began by dramatizing stories of his pioneer ancestors; then, in 1912, four years after his first trip to the Great Plains, he published his best-known book, *Riders of the Purple Sage.* Like Owen Wister's *Virginian, Riders* is a melodrama centering on a rough gunman hero—a man who is almost an outlaw in some ways, but whose moral code leads him to do the right thing. And like *The Virginian,* Grey's book inspired many imitators. Zane Grey and other writers of western adventure stories and melodramas also fed the growing appetite for western movies: scores of films were made from Grey's works alone. This excerpt from the final chapter of *Riders of the Purple Sage* opens with Lassiter, the hero, guiding a beautiful young Mormon woman into the wilderness to save her from cruel pursuers led by a villain named Tull.

AT HIS BIDDING she mounted and rode on close to the heels of his burro. The canyon narrowed; the walls lifted their rugged rims higher; and the sun shone down hot from the center of the blue stream of sky above. Lassiter traveled slower, with more exceeding care as to the ground he chose, and he kept speaking low to the dogs. They were now hunting-dogs—keen, alert, suspicious, sniffing the warm breeze. The monotony of the yellow walls broke in change of color and smooth surface, and the rugged outline of rims grew craggy. Splits appeared in deep breaks, and gorges running at right angles, and then the Pass opened wide at a junction of intersecting canyons.

Lassiter dismounted, led his burro, called the dogs close, and proceeded at snail pace through dark masses of rock and dense thickets under the left wall. Long he watched and listened before venturing to cross the mouths of side canyons. At length he halted, tied his burro, lifted a warning hand to Jane, and then slipped away among the boulders, and, followed by the stealthy dogs, disappeared from sight. The time he remained absent was neither short nor long to Jane Withersteen.

When he reached her side again he was pale, and his lips were set in a hard line, and his gray eyes glittered coldly. Bidding her dismount, he led the burros into a covert of stones and cedars, and tied them.

"Jane, I've run into the fellers I've been lookin' for, an' I'm goin' after them," he said.

"Why?" she asked.

"I reckon I won't take time to tell you."

"Couldn't we slip by without being seen?"

"Likely enough. But that ain't my game. An' I'd like to know, in case I don't come back, what you'll do."

At his home on California's Catalina Island in 1930, Zane Grey works on another tale of good versus evil in a Wild West setting. Grey's many westerns remain popular today.

"What can I do?"

"I reckon you can go back to Tull. Or stay in the Pass an' be taken off by rustlers. Which'll you do?"

"I don't know. I can't think very well. But I believe I'd rather be taken off by rustlers."

Lassiter sat down, put his head in his hands, and remained for a few moments in what appeared to be deep and painful thought. When he lifted his face it was haggard, lined, cold as sculptured marble.

"I'll go. I only mentioned that chance of my not comin' back. I'm pretty sure to come."

"Need you risk so much? Must you fight more? Haven't you shed enough blood?"

". . . mercy an' goodness, . . . though they're the grand things in human nature, can't be lived up to on this Utah border."

"I'd like to tell you why I'm goin'," he continued, in coldness he had seldom used to her. She remarked it, but it was the same to her as if he had spoken with his old gentle warmth. "But I reckon I won't. Only, I'll say that mercy an' goodness, such as is in you, though they're the grand things in human nature, can't be lived up to on this Utah border. Life's hell out here. You think—or you used to think—that your religion made this life heaven. Mebbe them scales on your eyes has dropped now. Jane, I wouldn't have you no different, an' that's why I'm going to try to hide you somewhere in this Pass. I'd like to hide many more women, for I've come to see there are more like you among your people. An' I'd like you to see jest how hard an' cruel this border life is. It's bloody. You'd think churches an' churchmen would make it better. They make it worse. You give names to things—bishops, elders, ministers, Mormonism, duty, faith, glory. You dream—or you're driven mad. I'm a man, an' I know. I name fanatics, followers, blind women, oppressors, thieves, ranchers, rustlers, riders. An' we have—what you've lived through these last months. It can't be helped. But it can't last always. An' remember this—some day the border'll be better, cleaner, for the ways of men like Lassiter!"

She saw him shake his tall form erect, look at her strangely and steadfastly, and then, noiselessly, stealthily slip away amid the rocks and trees. Ring and Whitie, not being bidden to follow, remained with Jane. She felt extreme weariness, yet somehow it did not seem to be of her body. And she sat down in the shade and tried to think. She saw a creeping lizard, cactus flowers, the drooping burros, the resting dogs, an eagle high over a yellow crag. Once the meanest flower, a color, the flight of the bee, or any living thing had given her deepest joy. Lassiter had gone off, yielding to his incurable blood lust, probably to his own death; and she was sorry, but there was no feeling in her sorrow.

Suddenly from the mouth of the canyon just beyond her rang out a clear, sharp report of a rifle. Echoes clapped. Then followed a piercingly high yell of anguish, quickly breaking. Again echoes clapped, in grim imitation. Dull revolver shots—hoarse yells—pound of hoofs—shrill neighs of horses—commingling of echoes—and again silence! Lassiter must be busily engaged, thought Jane, and no chill trembled over her, no blanching tightened her skin. Yes, the border was a bloody place. But life had always been bloody. Men were bloodspillers. Phases of the history of the world flashed through her mind—Greek and Roman wars, dark, mediaeval times, the crimes in the name of religion. On sea, on land, everywhere—shooting, stabbing, cursing, clashing, fighting men! Greed, power, oppression, fanaticism, love, hate, revenge, justice, freedom—for these, men killed one another.

—*Zane Grey,* Riders of the Purple Sage: A Novel. *New York: Harper, 1912.*

THINK ABOUT THIS

1. How would you describe Lassiter?

2. How would you describe Jane Withersteen's emotional state?

3. Can you summarize Lassiter's lengthy outburst about border life? Do you agree with him and with his course of action?

W. S. Hart's "Big Discovery": From Stage to Movies

William S. Hart, an easterner who had lived in the West for part of his life, was a stage actor known for his appearances in everything from Shakespeare to melodramas. In 1911, as he describes in this passage from his autobiography, he had an experience that gave a whole new direction to his career—and to the history of American films. Hart went on to star in many western films. To his generation he was as famous, and as closely associated with westerns, as John Wayne and Roy Rogers were to later generations.

WHILE PLAYING IN CLEVELAND, I attended a picture show. I saw a Western picture. It was awful! I talked with the manager of the theater and he told me it was one of the best Westerns he had ever had. None of the impossibilities or libels on the West meant anything to him—it was drawing the crowds. The fact that the sheriff was dressed and characterized as a sort of cross between a Wisconsin wood-chopper and a Gloucester fisherman was unknown to him. I did not seek to enlighten him. I was seeking information. In fact, I was so sure that I had made a big discovery that I was frightened that some one would read my mind and find it out.

Here were reproductions of the Old West being seriously presented to the public—in almost a burlesque manner—and they were successful. It made me tremble to think of it. I was an actor and I knew the West. . . . The opportunity that I had been waiting for years to come was knocking at my door.

Hundreds of ideas seemed to rush in from every direction. . . . Rise or fall, sink or swim, I had to bend every endeavor to get a chance to make Western motion pictures. . . . I was a part of the West—it was my boyhood home— it was in my blood. I had a thorough training as an actor. I was considered the outstanding portrayer of Western roles everywhere on the American stage.

"Rise or fall, sink or swim, I had to bend every endeavor to get a chance to make Western motion pictures."

It was the big opportunity that a most high Power, chance, or fixed law had schooled me for. It had been many years in coming, but it was here. And I would go through hell on three pints of water before I would acknowledge defeat.

—*William S. Hart,* My Life in East and West. *Boston: Houghton Mifflin, 1929.*

THINK ABOUT THIS

1. Why did Hart find the western film he viewed so awful?
2. What did Hart mean by the statement "It was the big opportunity that a most high Power, chance, or fixed law had schooled me for"?

Time Line

1843

Large-scale migration of settlers to the Far West begins.

1847

The Mormons begin their migration into Utah.

1848

After the Mexican War, the United States acquires California and the Southwest. The California gold rush begins.

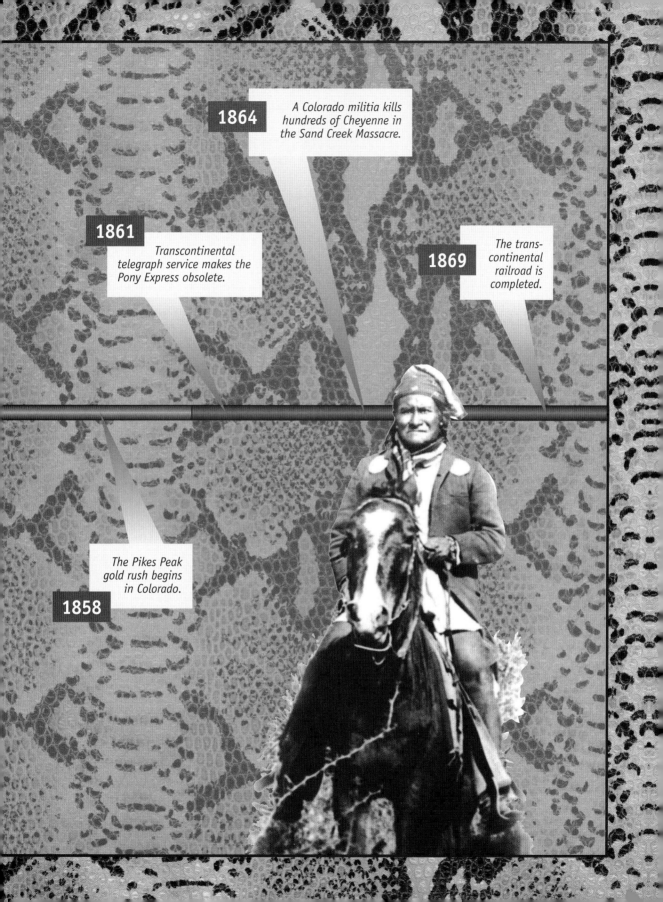

1881 A shoot-out takes place at the OK Corral in Tombstone, Arizona.

1890 The Battle of Wounded Knee Creek brings the Indian Wars to a close.

1886–1887 Severe weather on the Great Plains kills a high percentage of the region's cattle.

1892 In Wyoming, the Johnson County War pits cattle-company enforcers against small homesteaders.

1883 Buffalo Bill's Wild West Show opens in Nebraska.

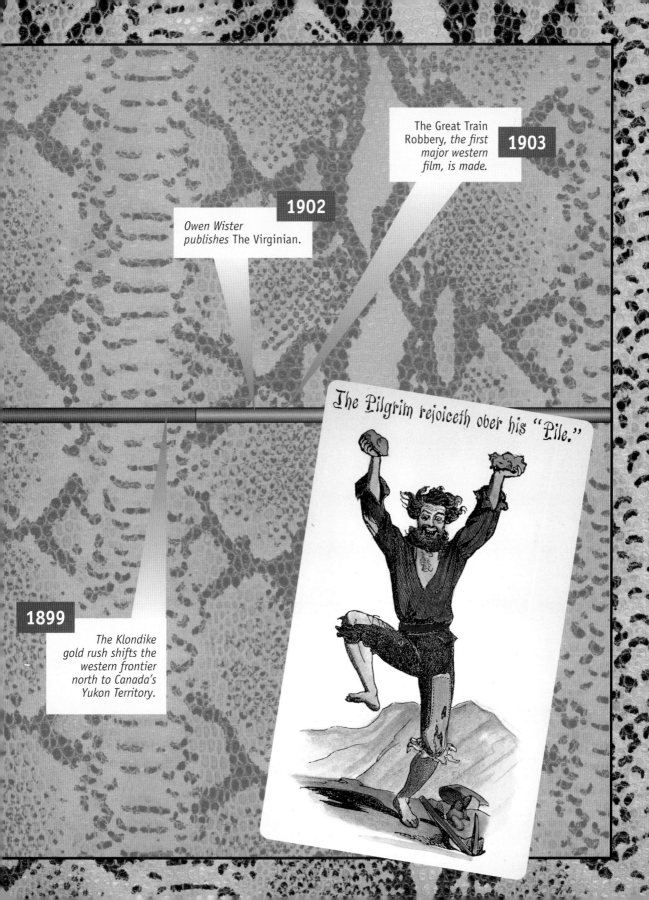

1903

The Great Train Robbery, *the first major western film, is made.*

1902

Owen Wister publishes The Virginian.

1899

The Klondike gold rush shifts the western frontier north to Canada's Yukon Territory.

The Pilgrim rejoiceth over his "Pile."

If any one person deserves to be seen as a symbol of the Wild West, it's William "Buffalo Bill" Cody. First he lived the reality, and then he made the myth.

Glossary

conflagration a fire

coulée a gully or dry streambed

cupidity greed

heterogeneous mixed

libels malicious lies

mortality death rate

plethoric full

speculator an investor, usually one who buys land and resells it at a profit

transcontinental reaching from one side of the continent to the other

vaquero a Mexican cowboy

vigilance protective watchfulness

To Find Out More

BOOKS

Alter, Judith. *Growing Up in the Old West.* New York: Franklin Watts, 1989.

Doherty, Kieran. *Explorers, Missionaries, Trappers: Trailblazers of the West.* Minneapolis: Oliver Press, 2000.

Duncan, Dayton. *People of the West.* Boston: Little, Brown, 1996.

———. *The West: An Illustrated History for Children.* Boston: Little, Brown, 1996.

Flanagan, Mike. *The Old West Day by Day.* New York: Facts On File, 1995.

Freedman, Russell. *Children of the Wild West.* New York: Clarion Books, 1983.

———. *Cowboys of the Wild West.* New York: Clarion Books, 1985.

———. *In the Days of the Vaqueros: America's First True Cowboys.* New York: Clarion Books, 2001.

Granfield, Linda. *Cowboy: An Album.* New York: Ticknor & Fields, 1994.

Hatt, Christine. *The American West: Native Americans, Pioneers, and Settlers.* New York: Peter Bedrick Books, 1998.

Lawlor, Laurie. *Window on the West: The Frontier Photography of William Henry Jackson.* New York: Holiday House, 1999.

Marrin, Albert. *Cowboys, Indians, and Gunfighters: The Story of the Cattle Kingdom.* New York: Macmillan, 1993.

Moulton, Candy. *Everyday Life in the Wild West.* Cincinnati, Ohio: Writer's Digest Books, 1999.

Murdoch, David Hamilton. *Cowboy.* New York: Dorling Kindersley, 2000.

Sandler, Martin. *Cowboys.* New York: HarperCollins, 1994.

Smith, Carter, ed. *The Legendary Wild West: A Sourcebook on the American West.* Brookfield, CT: Millbrook Press, 1992.

Sonneborn, Liz. *The American West: An Illustrated History.* New York: Scholastic, 2002.

Stanley, Jerry. *Cowboys and Longhorns.* New York: Crown, 2003.

Stefoff, Rebecca. *The Opening of the West.* New York: Benchmark Books, 2003.

WEB SITES

The Web sites listed here existed in 2005, when this book was being written. Their names or locations may have changed since then. Use care when using the Internet to do historical research. You will find many attractive, professional-looking Web sites, but proceed with caution. Many sites, even the best ones, contain errors. Builders of Web sites often copy previously published material, good or bad, accurate or inaccurate. In addition, some Web sites promote views of history that responsible scholars reject. Judge the content of *all* Web sites with a critical eye. Always check a site's sponsor or creator. Is is a private individual? An institution or organization? In general, you are most likely to find reliable, balanced information on Web sites that are associated with universities, colleges, or well-known organizations. Compare what you find on the Internet with information from other sources, such as major works of scholarship or reference books recommended by your teachers and librarians. By doing this, you will discover the many versions of history that exist, and you will be better able to weigh different versions for yourself.

www.pbs.org/weta/thewest/ is the home page of New Perspectives on the West, based on the eight-part public television series *The West,* by Ken Burns and Stephen Ives.

www.americanwest.com has information about many aspects of the West, including sections called "Gunslingers and Outlaws," "Cowboys," and "Women of the West."

www.historynet.com/we is the home page of the magazine *Wild West,* with a number of articles available online.

www.thewildwest.org is a kid-friendly site with information about Native Americans, outlaws, and other topics, as well as a Wild West quiz.

http://gallery.unl.edu/ is the University of Nebraska Press's "Gallery of the Open Frontier," a digital photo gallery devoted to the history of the American West.

www.filmsite.org/westernfilms.html is a survey of western films from the origins to the present, covering such topics as performers, popularity, and plots.

Index

Page numbers for illustrations are in boldface

ABOUT THE AUTHOR

Rebecca Stefoff is the author of numerous histories for young people. Among her contributions to Benchmark's American Voices series are *The Opening of the West, Colonial Life,* and *The New Republic.* Stefoff is the author of the ten-volume North American Historial Atlases series, also published by Benchmark. Her other books about the American West include *Women Pioneers* (Facts On File), *Children of the Westward Trail* (Millbrook Press), and *The Oregon Trail in American History* (Enslow). Visit her Web site at www.rebeccastefoff.com.